Understanding disability:
causes, characteristics, and coping

Victoria Stopford BA, CQSW, FETC

Edward Arnold

© Victoria Stopford 1987

First published in Great Britain 1987
by Edward Arnold (Publishers) Ltd
41 Bedford Square
London WC1B 3DQ

Edward Arnold (Australia) Pty Ltd
80 Waverley Road
Caulfield East
Victoria 3145
Australia

British Library Cataloguing in Publication Data

Stopford, Victoria
 Understanding disability: causes,
 characteristics and coping.
 1. Diagnosis 2. Handicapped 3. Disability
 evaluation
 I. Title
 616.07′5   RC71.3

 ISBN 0—7131—3563—8

Text set in 10/11pt English 49 by Colset Pte. Ltd., Singapore.
Printed in Great Britain by Richard Clay (The Chaucer Press) Ltd, Bungay, Suffolk.

Contents

Introduction

The information in this handbook is primarily geared towards students and professional groups concerned with social-care work. However, the basic data will be helpful to anyone involved with children or adults with special needs.

Sections on a wide range of physical and mental handicaps are grouped according to the general classification of the disorders concerned — neurological disorders, neuro-muscular disorders, and so on. The index provides sufficient cross-reference to enable most information to be located within the sections. This book does not offer a comprehensive account of all disabilities, but, as well as dealing with the more common ones, it does provide information on a range of less well-known conditions where very often professionals lack up-to-date knowledge and understanding. It should enable students to gain a broad understanding of the different handicaps and their diagnostic categories. The book should also be a valuable source of information for project work. Information concerning voluntary support agencies and further reading material is provided at the end of each section.

The basic information given under each subheading provides sufficient scope to prompt insight and understanding into the way in which a condition may affect the whole family.

It is important to remember that severity within each disability is but one of many factors which will affect the way in which an individual is handicapped by a condition. Different individuals will face different problems, and many limitations are socially created. There is thus an obvious danger in making generalisations concerning all people with a certain physical disability, and lists of facts such as those offered in the following sections may inadvertently give a false impression of uniformity.

Many of the self-help organisations have tended to produce literature which gives an optimistic view of the related handicaps but which, at the same time, may support the rather traditional medical views found in society. Certainly these organisations are often the experts concerning a particular disability and can provide a forum through which can be established a national pattern of current problems experienced by families, management and treatment techniques, innovation, and research — at a regional level, one may find variations in opinion, treatment, and attitudes in both the health and the community services. Organisations are the experts largely because their information includes personal experience from those who are having to live with a disability. This pooling of facts, feelings, and ideas can support the often unrecognised need for disabled people also to achieve basic human rights. Thus professionals can learn from 'the experts' and in so doing encourage a working together of professionals and people with a disability.

The psycho-social aspects of coping with disability, in particular, have similar implications for many or all disabilities. An example would be the anxiety, confusion, and frustration experienced by a family before and following diagnosis of a particular condition. Support to the family by the medical consultant, general practitioner, nurse, health visitor, social worker, and other professionals may be crucial. Professional help may also be required at certain potentially traumatic points in life such as starting school, leaving school and entering employment, marriage, birth of one's own children where genetic implications exist, and so on. Some of these broader issues are considered in the chapter 'Chronic disability and self-image'.

Where especially relevant, a number of aids, specialist organisations, or training courses may be mentioned in a particular section. Some of this information may, of course, be of general relevance to other disabilities.

Physical disability is not easy to define, as there is an inevitable overlap with intellectual and emotional handicaps. For the purposes of this book, disability has been limited to physical and mental handicap and does not specifically deal with those conditions which primarily cause emotional handicaps or which can be viewed solely as a chronic illness. For most of the conditions chosen there is a supporting self-help organisation, and I owe a great deal of thanks to these for the time and advice they have given me in the drawing up of each section. These are as follows:

- Alzheimer's Disease Society,
- Arthritis Care,
- The Arthritis and Rheumatism Council,
- Association to Combat Huntington's Chorea,
- Association for Spina Bifida and Hydrocephalus,
- Asthma Society and Friends of the Asthma Research Council,
- British Association of Myasthenics,
- British Diabetic Association,
- British Dyslexia Association,
- British Heart Foundation,

- The British Polio Fellowship,
- Brittle Bone Society,
- The Chest, Heart and Stroke Association,
- The Coeliac Society,
- The Cystic Fibrosis Research Trust,
- Down's Syndrome Association,
- Friedreich's Ataxia Group,
- The Haemophilia Society,
- Helen Arkell Dyslexia Centre,
- Invalid Children's Aid Association,
- The Leukaemia Care Society,
- Motor Neurone Disease Association,
- The Multiple Sclerosis Society,
- Muscular Dystrophy Group of Great Britain and Northern Ireland,
- The National Ankylosing Spondylitis Society,
- National Association for the Relief of Paget's Disease,
- The National Autistic Society,
- National Eczema Society,
- The National Society for Epilepsy,
- The National Society for Phenylketonuria and Allied Disorders Limited,
- Parkinson's Disease Society,
- The Psoriasis Association,
- Royal National Institute for the Blind,
- Royal National Institute for the Deaf,
- SENSE,
- Sickle Cell Society,
- The Spastics Society,
- Spinal Injuries Association,
- Tuberous Sclerosis Association of Great Britain.

In addition I would like to thank the paediatrician Dr Ruth Vincent-Kemp MRCS, LRCP, DCH, MPS, who kindly reviewed and made comments on each section, and Mr N. Stewart for his assistance with the graphics. Figures 7 and 8 are reproduced by kind permission of The Royal Association in aid of the Deaf and Dumb and The Royal National Institute for the Deaf respectively.

Victoria Stopford

Genetic inheritance

Reference is made to inheritance factors where appropriate in each section. This may require some basic explanation, as follows.

Heredity is the principle on which various aspects of body form and structure and physical or mental activity are transmitted from parent to child. Certain defects, vulnerabilities, and specific disabilities can thus also be inherited from one generation to another.

Each inherited characteristic is controlled by a gene located on one of the 23 pairs of chromosomes which are found in the nucleus of all the cells which make up an individual.

Genes may mutate — i.e. change — spontaneously. Occasionally a gene mutation may result in a person acquiring an 'inherited' condition without any previous family history of it. This will then be passed on to any subsequent children of the person in the usual way for that condition.

Hereditary factors can be passed on in several different ways:

- Disorders which are caused by a dominant gene are comparatively rare — Huntington's chorea is an example. All those who are born with the dominant gene will develop the condition, and there is a 1 in 2 chance of each of their children being affected.
- Where conditions are passed on through a recessive gene — in cystic fibrosis, for example — a child will show the disorder only if *both* parents carry the recessive gene. If only one parent carries the recessive gene, then the child will be a 'carrier' — he or she will not be affected by the disorder but can pass the condition on to the next generation. There are many recessive genes in the population at any one time, but the chance of two carriers of the same genetic condition meeting is relatively small.
- Sex-linked inheritance of a condition, such as in haemophilia, provides that the woman carries the unfavourable gene but is unaffected herself (i.e. she is a carrier). There is a 1 in 2 chance of each of her sons having the condition and also a 1 in 2 chance of each of her daughters being a carrier of the condition. A man with haemophilia passes carrier status on to all of his daughters, but none of his

sons will be affected. The mutation of the gene originally occurred spontaneously, and thus for some families haemophilia may occasionally occur in a boy with no evidence of the mother being a carrier and no family history.

Of the 23 pairs of chromosomes in each cell, one pair are known as sex chromosomes (either two X chromosomes in women or an X and a Y chromosome in men). The other 22 pairs are known as autosomes, and inheritance controlled by these chromosomes is thus referred to as 'autosomal'.

An inherited inability to resist certain diseases may result in a person having a tendency to develop a certain condition — rheumatism, tuberculosis, and certain skin diseases, for example. Similarly, faults in the structure of certain organs may be inherited, resulting in a vulnerability in some families to certain conditions — for example, diabetes, asthma, etc. For these a 'familial' disposition may be apparent.

Abnormalities of chromosomes may arise due to accidental faults occurring during division of the germ cells involved in reproduction. Such congenital abnormalities are not usually inherited beyond one generation — in Down's syndrome, for example.

Chronic disability and self-image

There is a tendency to use the terms 'handicap' and 'disability' interchangeably and often to relate these only to a person who has a severe and obvious condition. The distinction between handicap and disability is defined by the United Nations, after the World Health Organisation, as follows:

- *Handicap* 'A function of the relationship between disabled persons and their environment . . . Handicap is the loss or limitation of opportunities to take part in the life of the community on an equal level with others.'
- *Disability* 'Any restriction or lack (resulting from an impairment) of ability to perform an activity in the manner or within the range considered normal for a human being.'

An impairment can be defined as lacking part or all of a limb, or having a defective limb, organ, or mechanism of the body.

Thus disablement is the loss or reduction of functional ability, and handicap is the disadvantage or restriction of activity caused by the disability. Handicap may be physical, social, or emotional.

Children learn to understand their own identity largely from the reactions and behaviour of others towards them. Responses within the family and from those close to them in the community are most important, but wider society may express other attitudes which are harsher, conflicting, or reinforce negative experiences. For children with a disability, the development of self-esteem and self-image may be based upon aggressive and depressive feelings concerning their own body image.

Lack of follow-up and necessary support to families at diagnosis of disability can engender feelings which hinder the important development of the mother—child bonding process. Many parents have commented on the professionals involved being reluctant to give information and clarification concerning a child's disability at birth. Parents may

1

also realise that there is something wrong with their child long before diagnosis is reached, which can be very frustrating.

Parents experience feelings similar to bereavement on account of their child's physical or intellectual impairment, and these may place additional stress on family relationships and result in particularly traumatic adjustment to and only partial acceptance of the disability. Parents of a disabled child sometimes experience mourning periods for the first two years or more, and these may seriously affect the child's view of himself or herself as a family member. Professional help needs to be offered at an early stage, so that parents can work through these feelings with counselling when required.

How much to tell a child with a progressive disorder is a difficult issue for both professionals and parents. There may be another child in the family likely to be affected, which creates additional stress. Shielding the child from the reality of the future and not allowing the degree of independence appropriate to other children of the same age may lead to difficult behaviour later on. It is usually more helpful if the child can be offered opportunities to discuss his or her own feelings and those of the parents and family.

Overprotection and guilt from parents contributes towards a reluctance by the child to relinquish the 'sick' role, which may in fact be encouraged by the family and society. Thus, consciously or unconsciously, the person remains passive in order to remain dependent on others. One direct consequence of physical disability for children is that they will be restricted or prevented from participating in certain activities. Such restrictions may result directly from the disability or may be imposed rationally or irrationally by adults or other children.

The effects of physical disability are not confined to functional limitations but include social and psychological consequences that stem from the reaction of others to the disabled child. Children with a disability generally receive less social and interpersonal experience, take less responsibility, are more protected, and have lower self-esteem than their non-disabled contemporaries. Anxieties such as fear of pain, bodily change, death, and loss of approval and love from important people in their lives may encourage dependency, loss of autonomy, and poor self-esteem.

Physical impairment and the treatment processes may be interpreted as 'punishment'. Many disabling conditions either cannot be treated successfully or offer no prospect of a cure. This feeling of being incurable can produce greater anxiety than the condition itself may warrant. Professionals thus need to encourage people's ability to assist themselves.

A boy of eight years with haemophilia was unable to walk correctly, due to a stiff left knee joint. When walking freely, it was noted that the child also used his left arm less easily and frequently, avoiding using

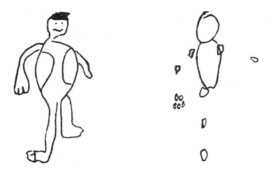

Fig. 1 How an eight-year-old with haemophilia drew himself

either this leg or arm when encountering stairs or climbing over objects. When asked to do a pencil drawing of himself, the boy drew his left limbs smaller than his right and with much less detail. When asked again to draw himself, this time indicating by a small circle where each of his limb joints might be, he completely omitted all joints on the left side with the exception of his elbow joint. For the following year, intense physiotherapy was geared to helping him become aware of his left limbs. This began with feeling and touching his left leg and foot and aiding the development of movement within each part. He was later able to walk almost normally, taking into account that his left knee joint had been affected by his haemophilia, and — more importantly — his body image became total.

Young children have a need to observe their physical state constantly, as they are concerned about their body image and sexual identity. Their identity concerning their place in society and their psychological and emotional growth are related to the degree of physical autonomy and independence that they have. As children with handicaps or disabilities grow up, the experience of feeling different and being different provides further complexities in relation to gender identity within the impact of chronic disability.

Young adolescents are naturally preoccupied with their own body, emotions, appearance, behaviour, and imaginary audience. These normal feelings have severe implications for young people with a physical impairment — particularly in terms of physical attractiveness, masculinity (or femininity), etc. Young adolescents with disabilities do not need to perceive that they are different as they have learnt that they are different. Gender identity may be further confused by, for example, a need to be dependent on a mother, leading to incomplete separation, or the influence of a hostile and distant father figure, etc.

Discrimination against adolescents can be for the best of motives. Their families may feel that they must be protected from the demands of the outside world and be shielded from the hazards of the environment which other members of their peer group have to deal with. Many adolescents who are disabled are seen as still needing an obtrusive 'minder'. For example, a young lad attending a mainstream secondary school was still being escorted to the school gate by a member of the staff to meet his mother.

Even in the best circumstances, adolescence can be painful and traumatic. Young people with disabilities will view themselves in the light of earlier life experiences, and the concept of identity as a young man or young woman will cause additional frustrations in adolescence. For example, the impact of AIDS or hepatitis on young people can be particularly destructive to their own level of self-esteem and identity in any situation where body contact is feared, and sexual relationships may be made fraught by the feeling of being 'untouchable'.

Undue protectiveness can unwittingly support the isolation of a child with a disability. Many youngsters are not able to participate in common activities such as sport, particularly in the school environment. Some will have been stigmatised by other children, and many will have lost time from school due to hospitalisation, visits to the doctor, illnesses, etc. A situation develops where integration into the non-disabled peer group may become impossible — yet conformity with one's own peer group is crucially important in adolescence.

With the emphasis on vocational, functional, and social integration — notably following the Education Act 1981 — the number of children with severe disabilities attending mainstream schools has acceptably increased. However, if transfer to a school for children with special needs becomes appropriate, the child and family need to understand the reasons for the change so that feelings of failure are not reinforced.

Independence is highly valued in our society and is associated with strength. Dependence is associated with weakness. It is difficult for young people to find privacy and independence if they rely totally on others to care for their personal needs such as washing, dressing, etc. The unfulfilled need for privacy and freedom of choice will provide additional frustrations to people in permanent care. The attitudes of people with disabilities to their own bodies may not be helped by an institutional environment where any number of people may be involved in the personal care of each person. Many carers may not allow people to attempt to do some things on their own, yet independence should be encouraged by intervening to assist only when required.

Those people who have been unable to make an acceptable adjustment to their physical disability are more likely to experience difficulties in coping with life in general and to have a low self-esteem and feelings of inferiority. Anxieties concerning their condition will probably dominate their everyday life and future prospects. Those who find employment are not necessarily those who have a less severely disabling condition but are more likely to be those who have experienced and developed a positive attitude to their disability.

Where the prognosis is poor, it is important that people are able to make career choices or continue in their places of employment regardless of the future implications.

People with a disability are often handicapped as much by the diagnosis and labelling which translates disability into something which society has to make provision for. It is easy for there to develop an assumption of perpetual limitation and a situation where professionals 'know best'.

Greater contact between professionals and families encourages an improved understanding of the problems involved. Staff are able to redefine their understanding of families' needs more appropriately, myths and misunderstandings are more easily dispelled, and relation-

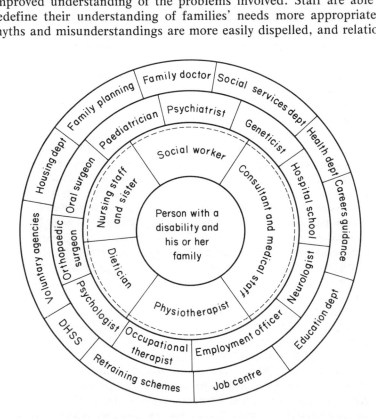

Fig. 2 Comprehensive model of the possible structure of the primary care team and support services required by a person with a disability and his or her family

ships between staff and families are less impersonal. Provision of detailed information and knowledge concerning a particular condition reduces anxiety and fear concerning present and future implications.

Many conditions require continuous medical support and management. Those hospital units which adopt a comprehensive care-team model involve the whole family in the treatment process and offer support to family members at any time concerning medical, social, educational, and emotional matters in addition to regular clinical reviews. Such a policy may at first seem to encourage dependency, but in fact it reduces anxiety and frustrations concerning treatment implications, provides mutual understanding, and promotes self-reliance. It is obviously important that members of the care team are readily available to participate on a day-to-day basis.

The growth of Independent Living Schemes (ILS) is significant for the future, as they support integrated living with an emphasis on equality of opportunity and full participation in everyday life in the community. Independence should be measured not by the physical tasks which can be done without help, but by the personal and economic decisions an individual takes supported by the necessary help. Having a place of one's own to live in, control over physical help, and additional necessary services, such as transport, encourages people to identify choices, make decisions concerning personal solutions, and take responsibility for what happens to them. This reduces dependency and gives social status.

The right to make decisions and take some responsibility for what plans and arrangements are made in the present and future is crucial to achieving independence and self-respect. For many people who are disabled — notably those with learning difficulties or those in residential care — it is not uncommon for others to speak on their behalf or make decisions concerning appropriate care and provision of facilities. The relatively new self-advocacy organisation in Britain (People First) has already made an impressive impact on adults with learning difficulties and has demonstrated how, by promoting self-advocacy, improved feelings of self-respect and self-esteem are related to improved body image and functioning. Such changes occur also in relation to the attitudes of others.

Conductive education, which was developed in post-war Hungary, uses a method of educating children and adults to overcome their handicaps, rather than just coping with them through the help of wheelchairs and artificial aids. The method has been practised in the UK on a limited basis but is now receiving greater interest. Children and adults are taught how to move normally by the rigorous, almost militaristic, repetition of small movements which build up to complex skills and gradually become automatic. Reinforcement through language is a crucial aspect. These techniques are taught by highly skilled therapists, and impressive progress has been made with people with Parkinson's disease, cerebral palsy, multiple sclerosis, spina bifida, and other conditions. Children considered incapable of independent controlled movements, having to rely on wheelchairs and specialised schooling, have been able to attend mainstream schools. Many adults with severe handicaps have been able to move back into independent living in the community. Thus control of physical movement can be an important aspect of encouraging independence and self-reliance.

The prevailing attitude in society has been that the disabled do not have the same emotional needs as other people. Society places great emphasis on sexual prowess and the importance of physical beauty, and this inevitably creates problems for those who are physically unattractive or who are sexually handicapped. Many young people with a disability grow up with unrealistic hopes of finding an able-bodied partner. Ideas of romance and love are equally relevant to a child with a disability as to one without, and opportunities to explore and experience the pleasure and pain of human relationships are thus important. In general, society's ignorance can be a major problem, but for the young person with a disability there is often a lack of opportunity to meet and form relationships with other people.

Marital breakdown is very high in cases where the onset of severe disablement occurs in youth or middle age. In situations where one partner becomes the carer, stress can be a particularly relevant factor in this.

Fig. 3 Obstacles to a better quality of life

Understanding the way in which a disability affects personal relationships, including sexual relationships, requires supportive information
and professional counselling. The implications and enforced changes
within a marital relationship place heavy demands on both partners.
Where these demands become overwhelming, it is often difficult for the
carer to remain supportive and not feel resentful of the commitment.
Respite care is a valuable resource to all concerned, and something
which professionals often underestimate. The inadequacies, impotency,
and changed sexual role placed upon a partner as a result of a disability
can be especially disheartening and difficult to rationalise. Thus
increased anxiety and poor self-image may be reinforced by future deterioration, particularly in progressive disorders.

From the above, it can be seen that children's developing self-image can
be seriously influenced by the way in which their families, the professionals, and society view a particular disability. Such attitudes affect the
way in which children accept or reject their body images and are also
related to their ability to cope with themselves, their limitations, and
their carers.

As has been suggested, several points in the life-cycle — such as
birth/diagnosis, schooling, adolescence, entering employment,
marriage, etc. — are particularly traumatic. How a family or an individual is supported through crisis periods and the extent and nature of
the resources offered will greatly affect the level of independence
achieved. Evidence suggests that a positive self-image encourages a com-
mitted and resourceful approach to life.

Useful literature

- *The meaning of disability: a sociological study of impairment*,
  Mildred Blaxter (Heinemann, 1980)
- *The handicapped person in the community*, ed. David Boswell and
  Janet Wingrove (Tavistock, 1974)
- *Handicap in a social world*, Ann Brechin, Penny Liddiard, and
  J. Swain (Hodder & Stoughton, 1981)
- *The family life of sick children: a study of families coping with
  chronic childhood disease*, Lindy Burton (Routledge & Kegan Paul,
  1975)
- *Better lives for disabled women*, Jo Campling (Virago, 1979)
- *Images of ourselves: women with disabilities talking*, ed. Jo
  Campling (Routledge & Kegan Paul, 1981)
- *A study of dependency in young physically disabled people and their
  family or friends upon whom they rely*, Ted Canrell, Jane Dawson,
  and Grace Glastonbury (RADAR, 1985)

- *Readings from mental deficiency: the changing outlook*, ed. Ann M. Clarke and A.D.B. Clarke (Methuen, 1978)
- *Looking at handicap: information on ten medical conditions*, Sarah Curtis (British Agencies for Fostering and Adoption, 1982)
- *Directory for disabled people*, Ann Darnbrough and Derek Kinrade (Woodhead-Faulkner/RADAR, 1985)
- *The disabled child and adult*, J.B.M. Davies (Baillière Tindall, 1982)
- *Disability rights handbook* (Disability Alliance, annual)
- *Stigma: notes on the management of spoiled identity*, Erving Goffman (Penguin, 1970)
- *Entitled to love: sexual and emotional needs of the handicapped*, Wendy Greengross (National Marriage Guidance Council, 1976)
- *Working together with handicaped children*, Margaret Griffiths and Philippa Russell (Souvenir Press, 1985)
- *The family and the handicapped child: a study of cerebral palsied children in their homes*, Sheila Hewett (Allen & Unwin, 1970)
- *Stigma*, P. Hunt (Geoffrey Chapman, 1966)
- *Coping with disability*, Peggy Jay (Disabled Living Foundation, 1984)
- *Behaviour problems in handicapped children: the Beech Tree House approach*, Malcolm C. Jones (Souvenir Press, 1983)
- *Handicap and family crisis*, S. Kew (Pitman, 1975)
- *Personal relationships: the handicapped and the community*, ed. Derek Lancaster-Gaye (Routledge & Kegan Paul, 1972)
- *A mentally handicapped child in the family*, Mary McCormack (Constable, 1979)
- *A study of physically handicapped children and their families*, J. McMichael (Staples Press, 1971)
- *Educational implications of disability — a guide for teachers*, Judith Male and Claudia Thompson (RADAR, 1985)
- *Employer's guide to disabilities*, Bert Massie and Melvyn Kettle (RADAR, 1983)
- *Your child is different*, ed. David Mitchell (Allen & Unwin, 1982)
- *The psychological assessment of mental and physical handicap*, ed. Peter Mittler (Methuen, 1970)
- *People not patients: problems and policies in mental handicap*, Peter Mittler (Methuen, 1979)
- *Getting through to your handicapped child*, Elizabeth Newson and Tony Hipgrave (Cambridge University Press, 1982)
- *Social work with disabled people*, Michael Oliver (Macmillan, 1983)
- *Parents as partners*, Gillian Pugh (National Children's Bureau, 1981)
- *You and your handicapped child*, Ann Purser (Allen & Unwin, 1981)
- *Abnormality and normality: the mothering of thalidomide children*, E. Roskies (Cornell University Press, 1972)

- *Handicapped children: a total population prevalence study of education, physical and behavioural disorders*, M. Rutter, J. Tizard, and K. Whitmore (Longman, 1968)
- *After I'm gone: what will happen to my handicapped child?*, Gerald Sanctuary (Souvenir Press, 1984)
- *The psychology of handicap*, Rosemary Shakespeare (Methuen, 1975)
- *The educational and social needs of children with severe handicap*, M. Stevens (Edward Arnold, 1976)
- *The experience of handicap*, David Thomas (Methuen, 1982)
- *The social psychology of childhood disability*, David Thomas (Methuen, 1978)
- *Social responses to handicap*, Eda Topliss (Longman, 1982)
- *Charter for the disabled*, E. Topliss and B. Gould (Basil Blackwell and Martin Robertson, 1981)
- *Learning to cope*, Edward Whelan and Barbara Speake (Souvenir Press, 1979)
- *We can speak for ourselves: self-advocacy by mentally handicapped people*, Paul Williams and Bonnie Shoultz (Souvenir Press, 1982)
- *Living with handicap*, E. Younghusband, D. Birchall, R. Davie, and M. Kellmer-Pringle (National Bureau for Co-operation in Child Care, 1970)

Neurological disorders

Alzheimer's disease

Introduction   Alzheimer's disease (AD) is the most common form of dementia. As with other forms of dementia, there is a progressive decline in the ability to remember, to think, and to reason, with an associated physical decline. In 1907 Alois Alzheimer, a German neurologist, described the changes in the brain which are characteristic of this condition. These changes result in poor functioning of a large number of brain cells.

Dementia may affect as many as 1 in 10 over the age of 65 years. It may begin as early as in the forties age group.

Main characteristics   There is a great variability of symptoms, and some may affect one person and not another. Whether the condition deteriorates rapidly, in a few months, or gradually over a number of years also varies.

Initially a person may seem apathetic, slow to grasp ideas, and find decision-making more difficult. People often become irritable and forgetful, and this can also contribute to an inability to adapt to change.

Later, memory is seriously affected; incontinence is common; and help and supervision are required for dressing, washing, eating, etc. Everyday objects, people, and places are no longer familiar. Extreme restlessness and agitation, especially at night, are common. Speech and mobility may become seriously affected too.

Causes   Alzheimer's disease occurs more often in older people and accounts for about half of all cases of dementia. Multi-infarct dementia is the next most common form of dementia and accounts for about a fifth of all cases. A further fifth have both kinds of dementia.

An infarct is a region of dead tissue caused by lack of blood supply. Multi-infarct dementia often results from a series of small strokes which

11

block the blood supply and damage the brain cells in a specific area. However the cause of AD is not known.

AD is not caused by old age, does not seem to be related to blood-supply problems, and affects people in all occupations. Stress is not thought to be a contributory factor.

Inheritance pattern   AD is not thought to be inherited, but there may be a familial tendency evident in some families.

Diagnosis   Onset of this condition is difficult to identify, as it usually progresses gradually. There is no clear test for AD, and diagnosis is made by excluding other possible conditions.

Sometimes diagnosis cannot be reached until the condition has been fully investigated over a long period of time. This can be frustrating for the person and his or her family. Ultimately AD can be confirmed only by microscopic examination after death.

Treatment   A good working relationship with the family doctor and guidance from a neurologist are vital aspects of treatment and care.

Some people with AD find that they are more vulnerable to other ill-nesses, which can contribute to the general confusion experienced.

In some circumstances, medication may be helpful in reducing the effects of the disturbed behaviour, especially at night.

Family living   Caring for a person with Alzheimer's disease or dementia can be a difficult and demanding task. It is most important that family members have adequate support and relief. Feelings of grief, guilt, frustration, and embarrassment can make the caring role especially traumatic.

The person with AD may be angry and frustrated concerning his or her difficulties and may deny the problems of confusion, disorientation, etc. Everyday experience may prove overwhelming and cause seemingly inappropriate distress. Agitation, anger, and anxiety are common reactions to relatively minor traumas.

Assistance with personal hygiene, dressing, eating meals, and super-vision in general may become necessary. Practical aids can help to deal with incontinence.

Wandering, particularly at night, can be of major concern to families. Aids to memory such as message pads, clocks, drawings, photos, etc., can be of value.

Social situations and holidays may not only be practically difficult but can also cause additional confusion. Day care at a centre or hospital can provide valuable relief to carers but may, at first, seem disturbing to the person with AD.

Support agencies The Alzheimer's Disease Society has local groups or contacts throughout the UK. A newsletter and information service are available. The Society publishes a very comprehensive and supportive booklet written for families and carers, called *Caring for the person with dementia*.

Social services departments can assist with a variety of services such as meals-on-wheels, home helps, day centres, residential homes, aids and adaptations, etc.

The Disabled Living Foundation can provide advice on specialised aids.

Crossroads Care Attendant Trust can supplement or complement care-attendant schemes available through statutory agencies, but this scheme does not operate in all areas of the country.

Age Concern may advise on local services and provide information, and the Association of Carers has a number of local self-help groups.

Useful literature

- *Coping with caring: a guide to identifying and supporting an elderly person with dementia*, Brian Lodge (MIND, 1981)
- *Our elders*, G.K. Wilcock and J.A. Muir Gray (Oxford University Press, 1981)
- *The 36-hour day*, Nancy L. Mace and Peter V. Rabins (Age Concern, 1985)
- *We never said goodbye*, Isobelle Gidley and Richard Shears (Allen & Unwin, 1986)

Cerebral palsy

Introduction Cerebral palsy is a disorder of movement and posture appearing in the early years of life. It is caused by damage to, or lack of development in, a small part of the brain controlling movement and posture. It has been described as 'a lively mind in a disobedient body'.

The term 'cerebral palsy' covers a wide range of types and severity of disability. Some people are so mildly affected that there may be no obvious disability: others may be very seriously handicapped.

Often the damage to, or lack of development in, the areas of the brain causing cerebral palsy also affects other parts of the brain, resulting in other types of disability, such as mental handicap, visual impairment, and loss of sensation.

Main characteristics   Cerebral palsy is a disorder affecting nerve supply of the muscles. There are three types of cerebral palsy:

i) If a certain part of the cortex or outer layer of the brain is damaged, spasticity is caused. The child with spasticity has tight muscles which reduce the ability to control movement, and this results in weakness. Spastic cerebral palsy is only one type of cerebral palsy, albeit the most common. It is thus inaccurate to refer to all people with cerebral palsy as 'spastics'.

ii) If the basal ganglia (situated below the cortex and in the middle of the brain) are affected, athetosis results. Features of athetosis include frequent involuntary movements which mask and interfere with the normal movements of the whole body. These involuntary movements occur all the time the person is awake, especially when attempts are made to make a conscious movement.

iii) When the cerebellum (which is at the base of the brain) is affected, the child has ataxia, which causes lack of balance and poor co-ordination.

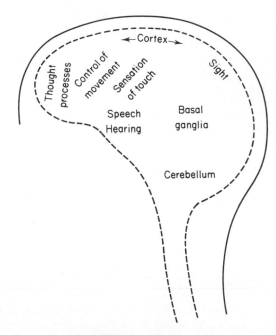

Fig. 4 Areas of the brain. Failure to develop or damage to the cortex may result in spasticism, to the basal ganglia may result in athetosis, and to the cerebellum may result in ataxia

Cerebral palsy may involve one limb (monoplegia); both the lower limbs (paraplegia); upper and lower limbs on one side (hemiplegia); mainly the lower limbs, but the upper limbs to some extent (diplegia); or all four limbs (quadriplegia or tetraplegia).

There may be many different associated handicaps, the commonest being speech and language difficulties, which affect almost half of those with cerebral palsy. Hearing loss, visual defects, sensation loss, convulsions, oral problems such as in swallowing or drooling, and learning difficulties may also be experienced.

Causes The incidence of cerebral palsy is said to be between 2 to 2.5 per 1000 births, without any distinction of sex, race, maternal age, or social background.

There are many causes, which occur before or during birth or within the first few years of life. They include

- German measles (rubella) during pregnancy;
- lack of oxygen to the baby's brain before or during birth — caused by factors such as haemorrhage at the site of the placenta, poor development of the placenta, or abnormality of the umbilical cord;
- incompatibility between the rhesus factors in the parents' blood;
- premature birth;
- disorders in the mother, such as diabetes or toxaemia of pregnancy;
- birth injury; and
- problems in later life, such as head injuries, viral infections (meningitis, for example), poisoning, interruption of the oxygen supply to the brain, and brain tumours.

Excess oxygen can cause brain damage and neurological defects in the newborn child. The volume and pressure of any oxygen administered must be carefully monitored. This is of particular relevance to pre-term babies.

Inheritance pattern Cerebral palsy is generally not a hereditary condition, and it is unusual for two cases to occur in the same family.

Diagnosis A child may be born with cerebral palsy due to problems in pregnancy, to brain damage at birth,or to an injury or illness during the early years. The diagnosis is often not made until the child is at least one year old, and the cause is very often not identified.

After they have left the hospital following diagnosis, many parents find that they have more questions to ask or matters to discuss. It is important that they feel able to return to the hospital team for assistance and that they know who else they might contact, such as the health visitor, the social worker, The Spastics Society, etc.

Early recognition that something is wrong needs to be followed by speedy and skilful assessment of the child's needs by specialists.

Cerebral palsy before the age of two to three years is very different from brain damage later, as people in the latter group have experienced some normal development.

Treatment   Correct treatment given early enough in life can often bring great benefit. No way has been found to repair the damage to the brain cells, but without skilled treatment the effect of the damage becomes more serious.

Education, training, and therapy can greatly help and can be the difference between a person being independent or being virtually helpless all his or her life. Most physiotherapy units follow an empirical method, selecting what works and what is necessary for each child according to the severity and type of motor disorder and other disabilities, and taking into account the child's developmental age. Therapists analyse the motor problems and work to maximise the child's functioning. This will also help prevent the development of secondary problems.

The Spastics Society offers an assessment service to people with cerebral palsy and their families. Advisory sessions draw upon an interdisciplinary team consisting of doctors, psychologists, occupational therapists, and social workers.

Diet and exercise   Children are encouraged to apply what they learn in physiotherapy sessions to everyday life. This can gradually help to train the child to use limbs as normally as possible. This is a long slow process which may need to continue into adolescence and even adulthood.

Swimming and horse riding can be particularly helpful forms of therapy. With proper coaching and encouragement, children and adults with cerebral palsy can participate in a variety of leisure activities adaptable to their individual disabilities.

The types of food chosen may need to include those which alleviate constipation, and which can be easily chewed or swallowed.

Family living   The family of a child who is severely or profoundly handicapped have to adjust to a routine of constant care and attention which will not change significantly as the child grows older. Other problems develop as the child gets heavier to lift, and there may be feeding difficulties etc. Parents therefore need to feel able to arrange for a break. It is also important that the child learns to relate to carers other than his or her parents, so that he or she does not become too emotionally dependent on them.

Respite care may be available through the social services department, or the child may begin to attend a nursery, day centre, or social-care centre. Parents may feel anxious about leaving the child in hospital or day-care provision as they may be the only people the child can communicate with. However, specialist staff will usually listen to the parents' instructions and try to co-operate where possible.

In the care and management of cerebral palsy, a number of community services are needed. These include, the family doctor and liaison with the hospital medical team, special equipment and aids, rehousing or adaptation of the home, home nursing, occupational therapy, home help, employment services, assistance with legal and financial matters, supportive counselling, etc.

As the child with cerebral palsy grows up into a young adult, it is necessary for the usual kinds of activities, hobbies, and social life to be available. These may include clubs, outdoor pursuits, and holidays organised for the disabled by a range of national and local organisations. The need to be independent and to form meaningful relationships with members of both sexes will be the same as for any other young person. It is important that the young person feels that he or she is grown up.

Many parents are concerned about what will happen when they are no longer able to care for their child who is disabled, and this needs to be discussed and planned for well in advance.

Mobility Children with cerebral palsy may need to walk with a walking aid or use a wheelchair. Correct prescription of mobility aids to meet individual needs is important.

Education Some children with cerebral palsy attend mainstream day schools. All children can attend schools provided by the local education authority, and these will include schools for children with special needs. Many children with cerebral palsy have impaired speech, but teachers can encourage children to take a full part in discussions and other verbal activities.

Hand co-ordination can be severely impaired, and thus the child may write with difficulty, untidily, or slowly. Some pupils may need to use a writing aid such as an electric typewriter, a microcomputer, or a microwriter. Some children may have difficulty perceiving spatial relationships, position, shape, and size.

Further education and training As cerebral palsy is frequently associated with other disabilities, it is important to identify unseen as well as the more obvious handicaps. In some cases cerebral palsy may be the minor problem, and another disability such as partial deafness, epilepsy (commonly associated with athetosis), or maladjustment may be more significant as far as the choice of career is concerned.

The Spastics Society runs a number of residential assessment, training, and further-education centres throughout the country designed to meet the needs of those with different types of handicap. The Society also offers a careers service to young adults which liaises with the local careers service and attempts to provide a realistic assessment of the individual's capabilities.

Employment   Several hundred young men and women with cerebral palsy leave school each year in search of employment. Most should be capable of earning their living with the necessary training and guidance, but the majority do not find work. A young person who requires a great deal of medical attention and help with feeding and going to the toilet — possibly together with additional problems — is unlikely to be employed in the open market. The Spastics Society provides some opportunities within its skills development centres.

Many students who complete FE courses find that they are offered employment at well below the expected status and pay. When a firm takes on a person willingly, there is a much better chance of success for both parties than when a firm is forced to consider a quota of disabled employees.

Aids and benefits   Equipment to aid communication, mobility, and independent living can make a tremendous difference to a person's approach to life and to the satisfaction gained from it.

Aids centres are useful sources of advice and guidance concerning a whole range of aids and gadgets to increase the independence of the person who is disabled and reduce the strain of management on carers.

The attendance allowance and mobility allowance are among several benefits appropriate to families.

Support agencies   The Spastics Society, formed in 1952, is now the leading organisation in the world for the education, training, care, and welfare of people with cerebral palsy. There are nearly 200 local groups in the UK. The Society has over 160 schools, residential centres, work centres, hostels, family help units, and day-care centres.

The Spastics Society's Family Services and Assessment Centre offers an information service; advice concerning equipment, aids, and toys; personal and family counselling; post-school facilities and information; educational and medical assessment; and vocational assessment, together with short courses and seminars.

The Society provides leaflets and literature on almost every aspect of care and management of cerebral palsy, geared to both parents and professionals.

The International Cerebral Palsy Society, founded in 1969, provides support and services within each country for people with cerebral palsy, and places an emphasis on prevention.

Compassionate Friends is a group offering counselling, help, and comfort to those who are coping with bereavement.

PHAB (Physically Handicapped and Able Bodied) offers social and recreational activities. There are often similar groups at a local level.

Disability Alliance can provide information concerning benefits and allowances.

Useful literature

- *Conductive education and cerebral palsy*, Ester Cotton (The Spastics Society, 1981)
- *After I'm gone: what will happen to my handicapped child?*, Gerald Sanctuary (Souvenir Press, 1984)
- *Behaviour problems in handicapped children: the Beech Tree House approach*, Malcolm C. Jones (Souvenir Press, 1983)
- *Getting through to your handicapped child*, Elizabeth Newson and Tony Hipgrave (Cambridge University Press, 1982)
- *Working together with handicapped children*, Margaret Griffiths and Philippa Russell (Souvenir Press, 1985)
- *Helping your handicapped child: a step-by-step guide to everyday problems*, Janet Carr (Penguin, 1980)
- *Daily living with a handicapped child*, Diana Millard (Croom Helm, 1984)
- *Paediatric developmental theory*, Sophie Levitt (Blackwell Scientific, 1984)
- *Conductive education for adult hemiplegia*, Ester Cotton and Rowena Kinsman (Churchill Livingstone, 1983)
- *Treatment of cerebral palsy and motor delay*, Sophie Levitt (Blackwell Scientific, 1982)

Down's syndrome

Introduction   Down's syndrome is the largest single cause of mental handicap and affects about 1 in 660 children born in the UK. It was sometimes referred to as 'mongolism', due to the characteristic facial appearance which resembled that of the Mongolian races, but this term is no longer used.

The condition was first described in 1866, by Dr John Langdon Down. In 1959 it was shown that the basic cause of the condition was the presence of an extra chromosome in the body cells.

Main characteristics   Down's syndrome can be identified very soon after birth because of certain characteristics which may be present. Not all children will show all of the characteristics often associated with

Down's syndrome, but the following are the most usual.

- People with Down's syndrome tend to be short in stature. The skull is often round and flat at the back, with no definite hairline at the neck. The fingers and toes tend to be short and stubby, and the hands and feet thick and square. There are distinctive creases on the palms and soles, and the handprints and fingerprints tend to be simpler than those of a person who does not have Down's syndrome.
- The eyes have a characteristic shape and may have epicanthic folds (folds of skin joining the upper and lower eyelids alongside the nose). Squinting is common.
- The upper and lower jaws and the bridge of the nose may be small, so that the tongue appears too large. This is exacerbated by poor muscle control. Sinuses may be missing.
- The muscles may be slack, making the baby appear floppy, and the joints may be easily dislocated.
- There may be an umbilical hernia, due to weak abdominal muscles, but this is usually corrected in the first year.
- The temperature-control mechanism is usually poorly developed, and similarly the brain and nervous system in general.
- The intestines are inefficient at absorbing vitamins and nutrients, and the liver at metabolising carbohydrates.
- The skin and lungs are frail, and the children are more susceptible to colds and bronchial infections. Catarrh (excessive secretion of mucus from the nasal area) can be frequent, resulting in temporary hearing loss.
- Abnormalities of the heart and circulatory system occur in about a third of children with Down's syndrome.

Causes and inheritance pattern   Usually, the nucleus of every cell in a person's body contains 46 microscopic structures called chromosomes. These carry the codes for every characteristic which can be handed down from parents to children. The 46 are derived from one set of 23 chromosomes which were originally in the mother's egg cell and a matching set of 23 from the father's sperm cell. Chromosomes vary in size and shape and form set patterns. They have been given numbers 1 to 22, with the 23rd being the sex chromosome.

In about 97% of all cases of Down's syndrome, the egg cell (or sometimes the sperm cell) contains an extra number 21 chromosome, and so, when the new cell is formed, the baby has three number 21 chromosomes instead of two. This is called 'trisomy 21'. The extra chromosome appears at the moment of conception and affects every cell in the body.

This occurs by chance, although the risk is increased with the age of the parents. When the mother is under 20 the risk is 1 in 2000; if she is over 45 the risk is 1 in 50. The risk when the father is over 55 years is similar to that when the mother is over 45 years.

In about 2% of children with Down's syndrome, it is difficult to identify the extra 21 chromosome as it is attached to another. This is called 'translocation' and can be inherited. In rare cases, the genetic error affects only some of the cells while others are normal. This mixture is called 'mosaic' and it would seem that those with mosaicism tend to be less severely affected, both physically and mentally.

Diagnosis   It has been estimated that only about 20% of those conceived with this condition survive to birth. Diagnosis is usually given at, or soon after, birth, relating to the appearance and the striking hypotonia (floppy muscles).

Parents sometimes find it less traumatic if they are told as soon as possible and are given information about the baby's condition and how it has occurred.

Treatment   Before the Second World War, nearly all children with Down's syndrome died during early childhood. However, with the development of antibiotics, surgical techniques, and the spread of central heating, life expectancy has been significantly improved. About two-thirds will survive the first five years and have a reasonable life expectancy in adulthood.

In the past, extremely pessimistic prognoses concerning level of attainment were given to parents. It is now understood that the range of potential ability is very wide, and that negative attitudes clearly lead to underexpectation and underachievement.

Most children with Down's syndrome have learning difficulties of varying degrees, but a great deal can be done both to remedy the physical problems and to provide mental stimulation. The maximum effect can be gained when stimulation is begun during the first year of life. About 60% of children with Down's syndrome are considered to be only mildly mentally handicapped by their condition.

Diet and exercise   As children with Down's syndrome are inclined to become overweight, diet is an important consideration. Booklets provided by the Down's Syndrome Association provide guidance on diet and health care, together with special exercises aimed at improving strength and co-ordination of the muscles and stimulation of the senses.

Family living   Parents often feel shocked and distressed to learn that their child has Down's syndrome, and explaining the condition to their family can be a difficult and traumatic experience. However, other children in the family can be amazingly supportive and share the concerns of the whole family towards the problems and crises of their sibling.

Every child with Down's syndrome is a unique person in his or her own right, and the potential level of achievement should never be underestimated. A stimulating environment and a positive attitude from those around him or her will enable the child to make the most of his or her potential abilities.

There is clear evidence to suggest that those children who are given early attention and every encouragement from their parents, who themselves then have a positive attitude towards the care and development of their child, are not always as severely handicapped as has been generally assumed.

Many parents find the support of other parents they meet through local self-help groups to be very important. In addition, the health visitor and family doctor can be vital sources of reassurance in the early months. Some children may remain under the care of the paediatrician, particularly if there are physical complications.

More areas are setting up a community handicap team which can provide a variety of help. Some social services departments automatically visit families after the birth of a child with special needs.

Respite care can provide parents with a much needed break, particularly if their child has behaviour problems. However, many children and adults with Down's syndrome are easy-going, sociable, and eager to enjoy life.

One of the major anxieties which parents experience is who will provide the long-term care of their child when they are no longer able to. With the current emphasis on care in the community, there is a growing amount of hostel-type provision in many areas as an alternative to long-term hospital care.

Education   Some children with Down's syndrome go to mainstream primary and secondary schools. At the other extreme, a few are profoundly handicapped. Most learn to wash, dress, and feed themselves and take some responsibilities as independent members of society. Many learn to read and write. About 60% are considered to be only mildly handicapped by learning difficulties.

Most children with Down's syndrome can be regarded as having a learning difficulty when compared with their peer group and therefore have special educational needs. Local education authorities have a general duty to seek to identify those children whose special needs require special educational provision. Emphasis is, however, placed on looking at the child as a whole person and on the need to establish a working partnership between the LEA and the parents.

The LEA's assessment is not seen simply as a diagnostic tool but as a means of understanding a child's learning difficulties, providing a guide to the kind of education needed and a basis on which to monitor progress.

Further education and training   Educational courses of different kinds are being offered by some colleges of further education, often in association with schools or training centres. Again, these emphasise the value of continuing stimulation and improving social skills.

Employment An increasing number of young adults with Down's syndrome find employment in sheltered worshops or adult training centres, and many are able to undertake work of a limited but practical application in open employment. Unfortunately, however, public ignorance of their potential often limits job opportunities.

Aids and benefits The attendance allowance is frequently appropriate, and claims are usually made just before the child is two years old.

Support agencies The Down's Babies Association (later known as the Down's Children's Association) was founded in 1970 by parents and professionals who felt that children with Down's syndrome were not realising their full potential. As the Down's Syndrome Association, it now has branches and groups throughout the UK, providing support for parents and information and advice to both professionals and families. It publishes guides for parents and other literature on mental handicap in general and Down's syndrome in particular.

The National Research Centre for Down's Syndrome was founded in 1981 by the Down's Children's Association in conjunction with Birmingham Polytechnic. It provides research and developmental assessments for children countrywide.

Mencap provides training at several residential centres and a Pathway Employment Service.

Useful literature

- *Down's syndrome: a guide for parents*, Cliff Cunningham (Souvenir Press, 1982)
- *Parents as partners*, Gillian Pugh (National Children's Bureau, 1981)
- *Helping your handicapped baby*, Cliff Cunningham and Patricia Sloper (Souvenir Press, 1978)
- *Down's syndrome: let's be positive*, J.R. Ludlow (Down's Children's Association, 1980)

Epilepsy

Introduction   Epilepsy is one of the oldest recorded human disorders. It affects people of every age, race, state of health, income group, educational level, and social background. A person with epilepsy has a liability to recurrent attacks of temporary disturbance of brain function, known as 'seizures' or 'fits'.

Epilepsy can take many different forms and can be due to many different causes. The condition is different for each individual, and the variety ranges from disturbances in consciousness that are scarcely noticeable to the outsider — such as mild sensations and lapses of concentration — to severe seizures with convulsions. It is not a form of mental illness or mental handicap.

Seizures are due to sudden disorganised discharges of energy in the nerve cells in the brain. Such discharges can happen to anyone, but in normal circumstances they are controlled by mechanisms within the brain.

The known incidence of epilepsy is about 1 in 200 in the UK; however there are some people who do not seek medical assistance who are not included in this figure. Therefore there are estimated to be about 500 000 people, including 200 000 children, in the UK with some form of epilepsy. Epilepsy can start at any age, but it most commonly starts in childhood and before 20 years of age, with a slight increase after 65 years.

Main characteristics   People experience epilepsy in different ways. A person may experience a slight loss of consciousness with or without a fall or seizure, and some may have seizures occurring only at night or early in the morning. There may be sufficient warning of a seizure to allow time to stop work and sit or lie down in a suitable place. Attacks may be regular but be fairly easy to predict, or they may be frequent, severe, and difficult to control.

Because there are many areas of the brain with widely different functions, many different types of seizures are encountered. A generalised seizure involves the entire brain. Partial or localised seizures occur when initially only limited areas of the brain are involved, but often these become secondarily generalised as the discharge radiates through the entire brain.

The most frequently seen types of seizure are as follows.

a) *Major fit* or *tonic clonic ('grand mal')*   The person falls with no warning. Muscles stiffen, relax, and then begin convulsive movements which may be vigorous. Froth or bubbles of saliva may appear at the mouth. The attack usually lasts for about two minutes. The person regains consciousness but may feel confused for a while. A short rest or sleep may be needed.

b) *Psychomotor attack ('complex partial')*   Only part of the brain (the temporal lobe) is affected by disorganised electrical discharge. There may be involuntary movements such as twitching, plucking at clothing, lip-smacking, etc. The person may appear conscious but cannot speak or respond during this form of attack.

c) *Absences ('petit mal')*   These can easily pass unnoticed. The person may appear to be in a day-dream, staring blankly or with blinking eyelids.

Causes   Anyone can have a seizure, but most people have a high threshold against seizures. For some people the threshold may be lowered by certain stimuli such as fever in childhood, flickering lights, emotional stress, sound, physical exertion, drugs, etc. In others, there may be an obvious cause of seizures, such as severe injury, birth trauma, stroke, or tumour (symptomatic or secondary epilepsy). There are sometimes associated physical, psychological, and mental handicaps.

For others, the epilepsy occurs spontaneously and depends largely on genetic factors. This type (idiopathic epilepsy or primary epilepsy) usually starts in late childhood, is relatively easy to control, and tends to cease spontaneously in adolescence or early adult life.

Many different metabolic and endocrine disorders may give rise to epileptic seizures — for example, low blood sugar, upset mineral content of the blood in kidney disease, etc. — but the seizures subside when these are remedied.

Inheritance pattern   Families are advised to talk to a genetic counsellor, as family predisposition to seizures plays an important role.

Where one parent has epilepsy, the risk of a child having the condition is about 1 in 25. If both parents have epilepsy, the risk is nearer 1 in 4.

Diagnosis   Diagnosis is based on a person's history of more than one epileptic fit. Blood tests help to check general health and to exclude metabolic causes for the attack. X-rays help exclude structural causes for the fits.

An EEG (electroencephalogram), which measures the electrical activity of the surface of the brain, provides information towards diagnosis. A negative result does not exclude the possibility of epilepsy.

Treatment   With modern advances in diagnositic and treatment methods, it is possible to prevent or reduce the frequency of seizures for most people with epilepsy.

There are some benign forms of childhood epilepsy which almost invariably remit as the child reaches puberty.

Primary generalised (idiopathic) epilepsy, which usually starts in late childhood as either absences or major fits, is relatively easy to control.

The more common secondary generalised epilepsy, which is due largely to diffuse brain damage, is more difficult to control and is often associated with other physical and mental handicaps.

Drugs are the mainstay of modern treatment, and neurosurgery is reserved for selected cases. There are a few anti-epileptic drugs which are commonly used. When taken regularly, drug therapy is effective in controlling fits and in reducing their frequency and severity. All drugs have side-effects, however, but these can be kept to a minimum by careful prescribing.

Success in treatment is related to the type of epilepsy, accuracy of diagnosis and treatment, co-operation and understanding from the individual and the family, associated handicaps, and social problems. Self-care is important, which includes taking tablets as directed, avoiding large amounts of alcohol, and getting regular sleep.

In 1969 the Reid Report *People with epilepsy* was published, and subsequently the DHSS inaugurated three special centres for epilepsy: The Chalfont Centre, Buckinghamshire, and Bootham Park Hospital, York, for adults; and a unit at the Park Hospital for Children in Oxford. These treatment centres provide a focus for advances in diagnostic and treatment methods.

Diet and exercise   Some people find that regular physical exercise tends to lessen the frequency of fits, but there is no general evidence for this. Participation in activities is usually encouraged, although the use of gym apparatus at a height and bicycling in busy streets etc. is inadvisable for some people. Swimming should always be supervised by an experienced swimmer.

Family living   The stigma of epilepsy has always been reinforced by fear, superstition, and misconception. People usually come to terms with their own attacks, but cannot always be sure of the reaction of others.

Only if the fits are very frequent will small children need almost constant attention. Certain conditions may bring on seizures — for example, illness (especially fever), boredom, and menstruation, as well as emotional upsets and irregular use of medication.

A young child with epilepsy may feel unhappy and confused if set apart from other children at home or in school. Teasing and ostracism are not uncommon, but the insecurity and resentment which this kind of situation causes will influence behaviour and emotions. Thus a great deal of understanding and support is needed to help the child and young adult cope with the difficulties that may be encountered.

Many seizures need no attention, but for the major fit it is important to

- ensure that the person is out of harm's way;
- cushion the head with something soft;
- loosen tight clothing;
- after the convulsion, turn the person on his or her side to aid breathing; and
- stay with the person and offer reassurance during the confused period.

For those who have regularly severe attacks of epilepsy, residential care may become necessary, particularly where there are multiple handicaps. Families may find this difficult to come to terms with, but adequate respite care can alleviate the pressure on carers. Overall, however, emphasis is on care based within the community rather than in large-scale residential settings.

Mobility As of April 1982, a driving licence may be granted to an applicant who has had seizures if he or she can satisfy certain conditions. In general, the intention is to allow driving licences to be granted to those people with epilepsy who on the basis of medical evidence have been free from attacks for at least two years with or without treatment. If they have had attacks during the past three years, they should have had these only during sleep. Applicants who satisfy the regulations receive a licence for periods of one, two, or three years.

It is not possible to drive public-service or heavy-goods vehicles if any fit has occurred since the person reached the age of five years.

Education Most children with epilepsy go to mainstream schools, unless they have very frequent seizures or their epilepsy is too emotionally disturbing. Children with epilepsy should not be assumed necessarily to have associated severe learning difficulties, as children with epilepsy cover the whole spectrum of intelligence. Nevertheless, many such children do underachieve at school. If, however, fits are frequent and remain uncontrolled over many years, some intellectual deterioration may occur. Children with such intellectual deterioration present many problems and require specialised help. Care and training in schools for those with severe and/or moderate learning difficulties may be more appropriate.

For those children and young adults who have absences or minor fits, learning may be affected by the interruptions caused by seizures which are not always noticeable by others. Sometimes children are themselves not aware of an interruption but may be confused by the lack of continuity in the lesson.

Further education and training There are only a few professions and jobs which are barred to people with epilepsy. In assessing suitability for a particular course or training, the nature and pattern of the epilepsy should be known and considered in relation to the career choice. However, the most important factors are the person's aptitudes, skills, and personality attributes.

A small number of people who have frequent and severe attacks may require sheltered-workshop conditions or specialised training at social-education centres.

Employment   In general, most people with epilepsy are able to work in their chosen field of occupation. In order to be successfully settled in work, those liable to occasional fits require the understanding and co-operation of employers and fellow workers, based on a knowledge of what to expect.

Aids and benefits   If the handicap due to epilepsy is severe, the attendance allowance may be claimed through the DHSS. Mobility allowance may be relevant if the person has an additional physical handicap which makes him or her virtually unable to walk.

A few children wear specially designed helmets to protect the head from falls.

Support agencies   The National Society for Epilepsy was established in 1892. Its Chalfont Centre offers a full range of facilities for the treatment and care of people with epilepsy, as both in-patients and out-patients. Short- and long-term accommodation is provided. The Centre has a resident population of 400 between the ages of 16 and 80+, and the Queen Elizabeth Medical Centre has specialist facilities including EEG and a monitoring service for anti-epileptic drugs.

An extensive range of literature and video material is provided for professionals by the Society, and a support service is offered to GPs and hospitals.

In addition, the British Epilepsy Association, which has several offices in the UK, provides a regular newsletter, literature, and identity cards. Scotland, Northern Ireland, and Wales have their own associations.

Useful literature

- *Epilepsy handbook*, Shelagh McGovern (Sheldon Press, 1982)
- *Children who have fits*, J. McMullin (Duckworth, 1981)
- *Epilepsy: the facts*, A. Hopkins (Oxford University Press, 1984)
- *Epilepsy reference book: direct and clear answers to everyone's questions*, P. Jeavons and A. Aspinall (Harper and Row, 1985)
- *Epilepsy explained*, Mary V. Laidlaw and John Laidlaw (Churchill Livingstone, 1980)

- *Epilepsy: a guide for teachers* (British Epilepsy Association)
- *Epilepsy and the family* (British Epilepsy Association)
- *Epilepsy and mental handicap*, Joan Bicknell (British Epilepsy Association, 1984)

Friedreich's ataxia

Introduction Friedreich's ataxia (FA) is an inherited disease of the central nervous system in which there is a progressive deterioration of co-ordination and muscle control (ataxia). Identified in the nineteenth century, it is characterised by unsteadiness.

The age of onset varies enormously, but symptoms usually appear between 4 and 16 years, although sometimes as early as 18 months or as late as the mid-twenties. The incidence is about 1 in 50 000 in the UK, and the disorder is thus not very common. However, improved diagnostic techniques may reveal a higher incidence.

Main characteristics FA usually appears before adolescence. It is characterised by clumsiness, shaky movements, and slurred speech, as well as weakening of the muscles of the arms and legs.

By their early twenties, affected people often need a wheelchair, and by their mid-forties nearly all are unable to walk.

People with FA are more likely to have heart disease and diabetes than the general population and, partly for this reason, life expectancy is reduced. Two-thirds show slight abnormality or weakness of heart muscle, and some people experience heart palpitations. Heart failure can occur earlier than average. Diabetes occurs in about 10% of people with FA.

Sometimes mild difficulties with vision and hearing are experienced. Curvature of the spine, varying in severity, is quite common — particularly for those who develop FA in early childhood. Also, feet have high arches from an early age. Difficulty in keeping feet warm, due to poor circulation, is an additional common symptom.

Intelligence is unaffected, even when the disability is severe.

Causes A number of other disorders of the nervous system may be confused with Friedreich's ataxia. Due to the wide range of symptoms, it has been suggested there may be several types of FA.

FA is a degenerative disease which affects specialised areas of the brain and certain nerves in the spinal cord. It is caused by an abnormal gene which only gives rise to the condition if it is inherited from *both* parents. The abnormality in the genetic code may be the result of an enzyme deficiency.

Inheritance pattern Parents who are carriers can pass on the condition to their children, but do not demonstrate symptoms themselves. Every child of parents who are both carriers has a 1 in 4 chance of developing FA, a 2 in 4 chance of being a carrier, and a 1 in 4 chance of not inheriting the FA gene at all. Many people thus do not seem to have any similarly affected relatives.

All children of a parent who has FA will inevitably be carriers.

Diagnosis Walking may be abnormal from the start, but often diagnosis is delayed because families think that the child is just clumsy. Unsteadiness first appears in the legs, with difficulty in walking and loss of tendon reflexes. After some time, clumsiness develops in the arms and hands and in the muscles controlling speech, causing slurred speech and increasing difficulties with articulation, handwriting, etc.

An electrocardiogram (ECG) may reveal abnormality of the heart muscle, a common symptom of FA.

Diagnosis is made easier if a brother or sister is affected.

Treatment Treatment can be given for specific problems — for example, insulin for diabetes and drugs to lessen heart palpitations or to prevent muscular spasm of the legs. Remedial surgery can sometimes be considered for the problem of arched feet or spinal curvature. Some 'alternative' treatments are available but not widely accepted by the medical profession as being effective.

Genetic counselling should be an integral part of care and management.

Physiotherapy and speech therapy may be helpful.

Diet and exercise Obesity will hamper mobility, so for this and other reasons it is important to be as active as possible within the limitations of the condition. Bed rest should be limited to a minimum. Swimming is an excellent form of exercise, and continuing physiotherapy is helpful.

A few people have found special diets helpful, but this is not universal and in general the value of special diets has not been proven.

Family living Regardless of the extent of physical changes and deterioration, there is usually a noticeable slurring of speech. The condition has no effect on intellect, and thus speech problems can be one of the most frustrating aspects of the disability.

Support in the home with daily-living aids is essential. Eventually assistance will be needed with washing, dressing, personal hygiene, etc.

There may be no known history of FA in the family, and thus it is a

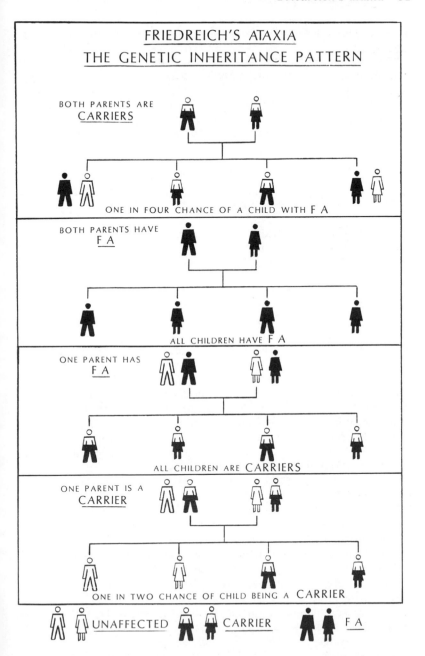

FRIEDREICH'S ATAXIA
THE GENETIC INHERITANCE PATTERN

BOTH PARENTS ARE CARRIERS

ONE IN FOUR CHANCE OF A CHILD WITH F A

BOTH PARENTS HAVE F A

ALL CHILDREN HAVE F A

ONE PARENT HAS F A

ALL CHILDREN ARE CARRIERS

ONE PARENT IS A CARRIER

ONE IN TWO CHANCE OF CHILD BEING A CARRIER

UNAFFECTED   CARRIER   F A

great shock to parents to discover that not only one but several of their children may develop the condition. Where there is a known family history, most families find waiting to see if their child will develop FA a particularly anxious and disheartening period.

Mobility   The average time for people to lose their ability to walk independently is about fifteen years after the first onset of symptoms. Generally the earlier the symptoms start, the earlier a wheelchair becomes necessary.

Education   Mainstream schooling is preferable, but the choice of school may be limited by the need for easy access by wheelchair. Certain technological aids can help overcome various difficulties.

Further education and training   It is important that career choice and training can be supplemented with the necessary aids and equipment. A great deal of support and understanding is needed.

Employment   Mobility is often a crucial factor, and it is helpful if the place of employment is within easy reach.

The Manpower Services Commission can provide aids to enable people who are disabled to perform particular duties of their employment which they would otherwise be unable to perform because of their disablement.

Aids and benefits   There is usually no shortage of available aids, but obtaining the right one is not so easy. An aids centre provides a useful means of trying out various aids and gaining practical advice.

Most families claim the attendance allowance and when appropriate the mobility allowance. The orange-badge scheme helps families to participate in and gain access to everyday activities.

Home-improvement grants and intermediate grants can be made available.

Support agencies   The Friedreich's Ataxia Group was formed in 1964 and promotes public awareness of FA, raises money for research, and assists families (particularly in an advisory capacity).

The Group has its own newsletter and organises courses for teenagers, 'talk-ins', and group holidays abroad. In addition, the Group has local contacts and groups throughout the UK.

Other relevant agencies include the Mobility Information Service and the Disabled Living Foundation.

Useful literature

The Friedreich's Ataxia Group publishes an information pack.

Huntington's chorea

Introduction Huntington's chorea is a severe hereditary disorder of the central nervous system. Although it had been previously recognised, George Huntington, an American physician, produced a relatively detailed account of the disease in 1872. In bygone years it was known as the 'dancing disease'. 'Chorea' means 'abnormal and uncontrolled movement'.

Onset of the condition is generally at around 30 to 40 years of age and it is usually fatal within 10 to 15 years on average. At least 6000 people in the UK are known to have the disorder, with up to 50 000 likely to be caring for a person with Huntington's chorea, being at risk themselves, or being a partner of someone at risk.

Main characteristics The most obvious symptoms are involuntary jerking movements, loss of motor control, unsteady gait, loss of concentration, and perhaps loss of memory (particularly short-term). Marked personality changes may occur.

Communication may become difficult as speech becomes uncontrollable, writing impossible, and thought processes confused.

Control of bodily functioning may be lost. Intake of food and drink becomes increasingly difficult, often with severe problems in swallowing. Acute restlessness at night may also be experienced.

Causes Huntington's chorea is passed on as a defective gene from parent to child. It is relatively uncommon, and few family lines carry the condition. Apart from the genetic aspect, the precise cause of the condition is unknown. Any person who carries this defective gene will inevitably develop symptoms of the disease.

The condition can begin at any age but usually begins in mid-life. The progress is unremitting, and the prognosis is of an unavoidable deterioration. Physical and/or mental functions may be affected — usually both.

Inheritance pattern Only children with an affected parent can inherit the dominant defective gene. There is a remote possibility that a gene mutation could occur, but this would be an extremely rare occurrence.

Any person in immediate direct line of inheritance has a 1 in 2 chance of being affected. The condition does not skip a generation but, due to the death of a relative at an early age from another cause for example, it may appear that the inheritance is not direct.

Those children who do not inherit the Huntington's chorea gene do not pass on the condition.

HUNTINGTON'S CHOREA
THE GENETIC INHERITANCE PATTERN

ONE PARENT HAS H C

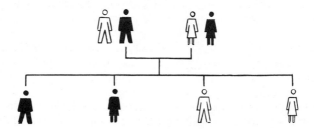

ONE IN TWO CHANCE OF CHILD DEVELOPING H C

UNAFFECTED   HUNTINGTON'S
                        CHOREA

Diagnosis   Three main factors in diagnosis are intellectual impairment, involuntary movement, and positive family history. There is no reliable predictive or prenatal test, and presence of the condition is established by observation of the symptoms. Recent developments in molecular genetics have, however, shown considerable progress concerning a predictive test, which it is hoped will be available in the near future.

Early symptoms are frequently mistaken for other conditions, and there may often be a long waiting period before Huntington's chorea is positively diagnosed.

Onset of the disease is gradual and insidious. The characteristic incessant movement is debilitating, and there may be an alarming loss in weight.

The person affected may initially deny any emotional or behavioural problems, but once the diagnosis is made it is important for the whole family to be involved. It is crucial too that all relevant professionals are informed, so that full support and assistance can be given early on. Families are often more willing to accept help at an early point following diagnosis.

Where the diagnosis was in doubt, it is always advisable for a brain autopsy to be performed after the death of anyone suspected to have had Huntington's chorea, to establish the implications for any children.

Treatment   Although each person will exhibit individual symptoms, and not necessarily all of those possible, it is usually inevitable that total nursing care will eventually be required. Modern drugs can alleviate certain symptoms, but there is no direct treatment of the condition.

Referral to a regional genetic-counselling clinic is not universal, but such counselling is vital. Support, guidance, information, and discussion are important aspects of genetic counselling, and all family members should be included. For those who choose not to have children of their own, adoption may unfortunately not be a realistic option.

Diet and exercise   As people with this condition tend to lose weight easily, a very nutritious diet is necessary (5000 calories a day, which is three times more than normal). To prevent choking or even suffocation in the more advanced state of the condition, it is usually necessary to mince food.

Family living   Huntington's chorea is a family disability, affecting everyone to a greater or lesser extent. Family breakdown is not uncommon, and often there is substantial financial hardship, social deprivation, and isolation. Personality changes — such as a lively person becoming lethargic, a placid person showing aggressive outbursts, a tendency to disorientation and wandering, or a disregard for other people's feelings and safety — come in addition to many potential dangers due to the inability to control movements (such as when smoking, lighting matches, and so on). Employment, marriage, insurance, and mortgage prospects may also suffer.

Children witness the deterioration of their parent and live in the fear of their own chance of inheriting the condition. In fact it is not unusual for someone marrying into a family to see a parent-in-law die, then nurse a spouse through a long illness, only to be faced with the care of one or more of their children.

There can be few comparable situations where fear is far more disabling and destructive than the condition itself. Fear of what may happen next and the inability to control body movements requires a great deal of understanding and support from others. Many find it difficult to adapt to change, and it is often preferable if a gentle introduction to residential care can be arranged when necessary. However, it is not always possible to find suitable residential accommodation for respite or long-term care.

For many families, the underlying attitude to life is one of no confidence. Such feelings of helplessness are also felt by the professionals. Anxiety concerning loss of self-control, 'madness', and dependency needs to be expressed and shared. A minority achieve a balanced and optimistic view of life, but all families require a great deal of help to adjust to the many points of crisis.

Mobility   A wheelchair can be used to aid a feeling of security and can be used trolley-wise to provide a support while walking.

Further education and training/Employment   It is important that the person remains in employment and/or training for as long as is realistically possible. Part-time work may be appropriate for the short term. The feared loss of career, self-esteem, status, and income eventually becomes reality. Many people find attending a day centre temporarily helpful.

Aids and benefits   Some aids and appliances are applicable to this condition — further information is available from social services departments. Family-aid schemes are also helpful where they exist. The Disablement Income Group lists general benefits. Mobility allowance is relevant in the later stages of the condition.

Support agencies   The Association to Combat Huntington's Chorea (COMBAT) provides a support service to families, information, a holiday and short-term-care home in Epping, and a social-work team which operates on a national basis to aid counselling. In addition to its national office in Leicestershire, a London office provides patient-welfare and family-counselling services.

Further information concerning holidays can be obtained from Holiday Care Service.

Useful literature

- *Huntington's chorea: a medical booklet*, D. Stevens (COMBAT, 1972)
- *On nursing Huntington's chorea*, Frank Gardham (COMBAT, 1982)
- *Huntington's chorea*, Michael Hayden (Springer-Verlag, 1981)
- *Facing Huntington's chorea: a handbook for families and friends*, S. Dalby, K. Evans, and R. Yale (COMBAT, 1984)
- *Living with Huntington's disease*, Dennis H. Phillips (Junction Books, 1982)

Multiple sclerosis

Introduction   Multiple sclerosis (MS) is one of the most common disorders of the central nervous system and one of the most baffling. It affects more than 50 000 people in the UK alone, and in some cases is severely disabling.

Formerly known as 'disseminated sclerosis', it is characterised pathologically by areas of demyelination in the white matter of the brain and spinal cord. This means scarring or loss of the fatty myelin sheath which surrounds nerve fibres and acts as a sort of insulation, resulting in inflammation and interference with nerve impulses to different parts of the body. Function is thus impaired in areas supplied by these damaged nerves. In MS, both motor and sensory nerves can be affected.

Main characteristics   The initial symptoms of MS may be weakness or clumsiness in one or more limbs, difficulty with balance, and spasms and cramp. Speech may also be affected. Blurring or complete loss of vision, paralysis of eye movement, and double vision may affect one or both eyes.

Where sensory fibres are affected, some symptoms may come and go, such as pins and needles, numbness, interference with vision, and insensitivity to heat or cold. Fatigue is a common factor, and varying degrees of incontinence may be experienced later.

Significantly, attacks may occur with varying frequency, severity, and duration. There is no fixed pattern, and no two cases are the same. A person may not be able to write, talk, sit, or stand up one day but may be able to the next when the inflammation has died down.

MS varies greatly from individual to individual, as well as from day to day for each person. It is impossible to predict with certainty how MS is going to affect any individual in the future.

The condition can be both debilitating and progressive, although many people may never become severely disabled and continue to lead reasonably active lives.

Causes   Multiple sclerosis is one of the commonest causes of disability affecting adults between 20 and 50 years of age. The age of onset is slightly earlier in women than men and begins at between 20 and 40 years of age in approximately two-thirds of cases, with a peak at about 30 years of age. It has been suggested that MS may be commonest in the upper socio-economic group.

It is clear that MS occurs in mostly temperate climates, particularly in the northern hemisphere. Incidence is about 1 in 2000 in the UK. It is virtually unknown in tropical areas, and rare in Japan and South Africa. There is some genetic predisposition, and geographical location, migration, and diet may influence the chance of developing the condition.

There is no known cause of MS, but it is thought to be a disorder of the immune response of the nervous system to infection by a variety of viral agents. A non-specific infection preceded the onset of the condition in about 10% of cases, but the infection may have been acquired many years before the symptoms first appeared. There is some evidence to suggest that, once present, the virus may be activated by infection, trauma, pregnancy, stress, certain food substances, or changes in temperature.

Inheritance pattern   There is no evidence that MS is an inherited condition, but a familial susceptibility increases the risk for first-degree relatives to about fifteen times greater than that in the general population.

Diagnosis   Diagnosis may be clear when there is a history of relapse and remission over a number of years, but there are many atypical cases which are difficult to diagnose. Because of the great variation in the course of MS, it is not easy to be certain of the diagnosis or the stage or state of activity of the disorder.

When a person is first diagnosed as having MS, he or she can experience shock, fear, anger, or even relief. As few people have knowledge of MS and its implications, patients may feel very frightened and uncertain about their future. Diagnosis comes at a time when people are young and often formulating careers, family lives, and personal relationships. Frustration of these may precipitate anger and bitterness. The whole process of diagnosis may be quite traumatic, and it is important that people know who they can turn to for support and counselling in order to cope with their feelings and isolation.

Some people may experience some of the main symptoms to a greater or lesser extent and their condition may not be diagnosed as MS for several years. This can be an extremely frustrating time for everyone concerned. The provision of accurate and positive information to people who have been recently diagnosed as having MS, and to their families, is crucial.

There is no reliable diagnostic test, but recently developed new techniques such as visual-evoked-response (VER) recording and quantitative electro-oculography will show early signs of damage to the optic nerve or the visual and oculomotor pathways, or impairment to conduction in sensory pathways. A lumbar puncture, in which a sample of fluid is taken from the spinal cord, can aid diagnosis, but both this and the VER test may be inconclusive.

Diagnosis usually involves the elimination of the possibility of other conditions which may produce similar symptoms, and is often predominantly based on a neurologist's opinion of the person's medical history. Many symptoms which the person is experiencing may be 'hidden' and quite subjective — for example sensory disturbances, fatigue, etc. — and very often people have difficulty in convincing their family doctor of the reality of these. In some cases it is thought that symptoms may be so mild that they are never brought to the attention of the GP.

Treatment   The lack of precision in diagnosis, the unpredictable course of the condition, the fact that there are remissions, and the lack of application of newer methods for measuring activity of the condition all present difficulties to trials of treatments and diets.

During periods of severe relapse it may be necessary to be supervised in hospital, where additional support, physiotherapy, and assistance can be given.

Physiotherapy can be beneficial when the person is experiencing muscle spasms and balance and walking difficulties. Use of the community physiotherapy services is preferable to regular visits to hospital, which can be tiring.

Counselling is an important aspect of care, and thus a link with the hospital or community social worker, or the health visitor, will prove valuable. In some situations more specialised help may be needed.

Drugs may be prescribed to relieve various symptoms, particularly during relapse. The ACTH drug is sometimes helpful for visual disturbances. A few people experience a high level of discomfort and may require pain-relieving drugs.

In general, a well balanced diet and periods of rest are important. A planned period of relaxation each day is recommended.

Diet and exercise   Any change of diet should be discussed with the doctor, but many people have reduced animal fats in their diet and increased polyunsaturated fatty acids found in foods such as sunflower-seed oil and Flora margarine. (The herbal oil of primrose taken with vitamins and trace elements will promote utilisation of the essential fatty acids.)

A few people have suggested that a gluten-free diet has made a dramatic impact on their condition and in preventing relapse, but there is no conclusive evidence in favour of this. Some people have found that avoiding certain foods to which they have become allergic has been helpful; but, again, there is no scientific evidence to substantiate that a change in diet can alter the disease process.

Excessive exercise is not recommended, but gentle swimming can be helpful and enjoyable, although some may be affected by the heat of the pool. Many find yoga a useful way of combining mental relaxation and exercise.

Family living   MS affects each person differently. Some may deteriorate physically fairly quickly; others may experience a slow decline over many years. However, it is distressing to all that MS often becomes evident in young adulthood when commitments to careers and families are most demanding.

MS affects the whole family, and the inevitable psychological and material adjustments required encourage despondency and lack of confidence. In some cases, emotional reactions are so strong that they can lead to severe emotional handicap.

Family relationships are often deeply affected by one member having MS. Children of parents who have MS are much involved in the situation, and information which is adapted to their needs is necessary. Support from family, friends, and the social services when appropriate is very important.

Fatigue is often a major problem — and one which others find difficult to understand. It can be made much worse by warm weather and hot baths. Reducing physical effort in daily tasks and in the work situation, in addition to regular periods of rest each day, can be helpful. The occupational therapist may help and advise.

An important aspect of family relationships which may be affected by MS is that of sexual relationships. There may be physical problems due to MS, such as impotence in some men, and a lack of sensation and mobility, and also incontinence difficulties, all of which can have a deep affect on sexual relationships. There are many emotional and psychological difficulties which can arise when one partner is having to come to terms with the fact that he or she has MS. Thus it is helpful if people know where to go for expert counselling and guidance so that neurological and psychological causes of these problems can be differentiated and solutions can be found. Certain agencies such as SPOD (Association to Aid the Sexual and Personal Relationships of the Disabled) may assist.

Mobility   More than half of people with MS never show an obvious handicap, but 1 in 5 may have to use a wheelchair. An American study of MS patients over a 25-year period showed that two-thirds were still able to walk by the end of the period.

Mobility may be difficult one day but get better the next, or may remain the same for several years. These ups and downs are difficult for everyone to understand and make allowances for.

Employment   It is important to continue life in much the same way as before diagnosis, provided time can be allowed for additional rest periods. If the work situation is very physically demanding, a different kind of employment may have to be considered.

Many people face the dilemma of whether or not to tell their employer that they have been diagnosed as having MS. It has been found to be beneficial to give employers accurate and positive information about the condition.

Most people are encouraged to stay in work for as long as possible or to take part-time work, as a healthy emotional outlook is important.

Aids and benefits   Recommendations for aids and adaptations to the home can be made via the doctor and the social services department. Continence advisors can give much help and information regarding the promotion of continence.

Medical confirmation of diagnosis is usually required before being registered as disabled and claiming DHSS benefits. Mobility allowance may be relevant.

Support agencies   The Multiple Sclerosis Society promotes research, sponsors projects, and provides a selection of helpful literature to families and professionals. Its welfare work is undertaken largely by its 350 local branches and seven holiday or short-stay homes.

CRACK MS groups are linked to many Multiple Sclerosis Society branches. They are geared to both the younger age ranges and the newly diagnosed. These support groups are informal, often meeting in each other's homes, and provide an opportunity to share problems.

Action for Research into Multiple Sclerosis (ARMS) will also provide help and advice. It provides a 24-hour counselling service available from main areas in the UK. Interest and encouragement is given to self-help, diet, and use of new techniques to help stabilise symptoms (for example, increased oxygen under pressure etc.).

SPOD (Association to Aid the Sexual and Personal Relationships of the Disabled) will also offer information and advice.

Useful literature

- *Living with multiple sclerosis*, Elizabeth Forsythe (Faber & Faber, 1979)
- *Multiple sclerosis: the facts*, W.B. Matthews (Oxford University Press, 1983)
- *Multiple sclerosis: a concise summary for nurses and patients*, Joan Atkinson (John Wright & Son, 1974)
- *Multiple sclerosis: a personal exploration*, Alexander Burnfield (Souvenir Press, 1986)
- *Multiple sclerosis: a self-help guide to its management*, Judy Graham (Thorsons, 1981)
- *Multiple sclerosis: psychological and social aspects*, ed. Aart F. Simons (William Heinemann Medical Books, 1984)
- *Multiple sclerosis and its effect upon employment*, Nicole Davoud and Melvyn Kettle (Multiple Sclerosis Society, 1980)

Parkinson's disease

Introduction   As 'shaking palsy', Parkinson's disease (PD) was recognised even in biblical times. In 1817, Dr James Parkinson published a classic description of the disease and established it as a clinical entity. It is a slowly progressive degenerative disorder of the central nervous system, affecting certain cells at the base of the brain. Once established, the symptoms may be mild, but they can increase gradually over the years, although there may be a period of time when they seem to remain static. Intelligence is not affected, and life expectancy is normal.

An overall incidence of 2 in 1000 in the UK affects men and women equally under the age of 60 years. However, the incidence increases to 1 in 100 over the age of 60. Parkinson's disease occurs in all parts of the world, but in developed countries, where people live longer, the condition is more common as it most often strikes in later life.

Main characteristics/Diagnosis   Three main symptoms are usually present to some degree for each person:

i) Tremor is not always present but, if it is, this slight shaking begins in one hand or one arm. It generally decreases when active or asleep.

ii) Rigidity or stiffness in the muscles is an early sign, and everyday tasks become difficult.

iii) Some people experience bradykinesia or slowness of movement plus a difficulty in initiating movement. Walking becomes an effort, and voluntary movement may be interrupted.

All these symptoms may appear very gradually, in no specific order. It may take years before early signs of tremor or movement difficulties become a nuisance.

Symptoms vary considerably in their severity at different times, and often one main symptom is predominant. Stiffness or rigidity is less obvious than tremor but is more incapacitating. Muscular rigidity — often accompanied by slowness of movement — causes the typical expressionless face, immobile posture, and difficulty in movements such as walking, swinging the arms, talking, writing, blinking, swallowing, etc. Tremor is worst when the person is at rest but disappears during sleep and is usually less during performance of a voluntary movement.

Some people find such difficulty in initiating movement that their feet become frozen to the floor when starting to walk, or they may come to an involuntary halt while walking. Similarly, turning around, getting out of a chair, or turning over in bed can be difficult.

Sometimes the stiffness of muscles is accompanied by pain. Balance is frequently affected, and fear of falling may severely restrict activity. In severe cases, people walk with quick shuffling steps with the body bent forward ('festinating gait').

The voice tends to become softer, and words may be slurred.

Dribbling is fairly common, caused by difficulty in automatic swallowing of saliva. A greasy and scaly skin may develop. Constipation is also a frequent symptom and is exacerbated by some anti-Parkinsonian drugs, requiring regular treatment with laxatives. Occasionally disturbance of bladder control occurs as a side-effect of drug therapy.

For most people, one symptom predominates. Although the severity of tremor is variable for different people, it is unusual for there to be no slurring or difficulty with voluntary movement.

Causes   The cause of PD is not known but it is believed to be associated with one small group of nerve cells in the brain (basal ganglia) failing to function normally. This affects the production of dopamine — a chemical substance involved in the transmission of messages between nerves and the muscles they supply — causing the muscles to stiffen and respond slowly or not at all.

The condition is associated with ageing in general and may be related to previous encephalitis (inflammation of the brain), or possibly follow a viral infection which very gradually damages the nerve cells.

There is no evidence of any link with diet or environment — although some have seriously considered pollution — nor is it associated with any particular occupation or social class.

Inheritance pattern   One in 10 people are known to have a relative with Parkinson's disease; however, there is no evidence to suggest that the condition is actually inherited.

Treatment   No one drug or operation will restore full movement, but there are various drugs which will reduce or alleviate rigidity and brady-kinesia and, to a lesser extent, tremor.

Various substances given by mouth are absorbed to alter the chemistry of the basal ganglia so that more normal functioning is restored. L-dopa a naturally occurring amino acid, is chemically close to dopamine and is necessary for its manufacture. Anticholinergics and other medicines also affect the chemistry of the basal ganglia and thus help to normalise the function of the nerve cells but they are unsuitable for the older person.

Depression or excitability may occur as a side-effect of taking L-dopa. (Depression is a feature of PD, although it may be in response to the difficulties caused by the condition.) Other side-effects of drugs include a feeling of hotness and a loss of bladder control. Hallucinations and nightmares are side-effects more commonly experienced by older people. After long-term L-dopa therapy, excessive involuntary move-ments (such as writhing) may result and there may be sudden on/off attacks in which mobility is lost for up to an hour.

These problems are very distressing, but a compromise has to be reached between an effective level of control of symptoms and an accept-able level of side-effects of the treatment therapy. Adjustment and change of medication in relation to side-effects can be made, but some side-effects are unavoidable despite careful adjustment. Regular check-ups at a special hospital clinic are essential, so that medication can be altered if necessary.

Formal physiotherapy teaches exercises which can be practised at home to help cope with the condition. Speech therapy can also be useful with respect to voice and speech control, feeding, and drooling, and communication aids may be appropriate when the condition is severe.

Future treatment methods may offer effective medication with fewer side-effects.

Diet and exercise   Natural exercise such as swimming, walking, etc. is important, as such activity, combined with the use of appropriate medicines, can help reduce muscle rigidity.

Vegetable fibre and roughage are necessary to help alleviate constipa-tion, and drinking plenty of water may also help in this. High-protein meals have, for some people, appeared to severely limit the effectiveness of drug treatment.

Chewing and swallowing problems may discourage eating, and this can be an additional cause of distress for the family. The speech thera-pist may be able to help.

Family living Many people with PD or their relatives wrongly attribute many of the symptoms to psychological causes. Neither the condition itself nor its symptoms are caused by psychological stress; however, anxiety concerning symptoms which are variable, hard to understand or explain, and frequently noticeable to strangers can itself make tremor worse. Tremor causes embarrassment, and the resultant tension will tend to aggravate symptoms still further.

Rigidity and slowness of movement constitute the most frustrating aspects of the condition. Slowness plus an expressionless face, possibly with involuntary dribbling, may give the impression of stupidity or loss of intelligence. People often feel that their self-confidence is undermined, and to be treated as childish or retarded tends to exacerbate this.

More time is needed for travelling, walking, etc. It may be difficult to be understood on the telephone.

Symptoms are often made worse when there is a deterioration in general health.

It is important for people to remain as independent and active as possible. Adjustments have to be made within the family, and this may mean considerable changes to the family's way of life.

Emphasis should be on care within the community, but domiciliary nursing may be needed to ease the burden on family members.

All the main symptoms can be helped by modern treatments, but drug therapy is at present effective only for a limited period.

Mobility Immobility is part of the condition. The family need to be tolerant of limitations and encourage continuation of an active social life.

Employment It is useful to seek adjustments in routine so that symptoms do not constantly interfere. More time is needed to complete tasks, especially those involving hand manipulation. A range of mechanical aids and other gadgets may be helpful — for example, a typewriter is often a useful writing aid.

Aids and benefits Occupational therapists within social services departments and hospitals can assess and provide advice on suitable aids. Attendance allowance, mobility allowance, and invalid-care allowance may be appropriate.

Support agencies The Parkinson's Disease Society collects and disseminates information to people with PD, their families, and professionals; provides a newsletter; and raises funds for research. Help (including a tape of speech exercises), advice, and in some cases financial assistance are offered, and a welfare benefits officer is available.

Special holidays are arranged. There are local branches of the Society throughout the UK.

The Disablement Income Group and the Disabled Living Foundation are important sources of information concerning aids and benefits.

Useful literature

The Parkinson's Disease Society publishes an information pack on PD and a comprehensive range of literature for patients and professionals, including *Living with Parkinson's disease*.

Spina bifida

Introduction   A group of disabilities classified as 'neural tube defects' is characterised by congenital malformations of the central nervous system. The most common of these disabilities are spina bifida and anencephaly. Spina bifida occurs when the spinal region fails to develop properly in the first 25 days of pregnancy. The fault can occur at any level of the spine but is most common at about waist level.

In general, spina bifida is the most common disability apparent at birth. The incidence varies from country to country and from area to area in the same country, with an average of 1.5 per 1000 in the UK.

Main characteristics   There are three main forms of spina bifida:

i) *Spina bifida occulta* is a fairly common form but rarely causes disability. It generally occurs at the sacral region and is usually only detectable by X-ray. In this type the skin is intact and usually the only exterior sign of spina bifida is a dimple or tuft of hair on the back. In most instances the nervous system is not affected, but in rare cases there is paralysis.

ii) *Spina bifida cystica* can be divided into two types:

  a) Meningocele, the less common of the two, shows as a sac or cyst on the back, rather like a large blister, covered by a thin layer of skin. The sac is composed of the meninges (membranes covering the spinal cord) which protrude through the bifid (split) vertebrae. Neurological abnormalities do not usually occur with meningocele, as the spinal cord itself and its roots are not disturbed.

b) Myelomeningocele is the more common and more severe form. The sac or cyst contains not only tissue and cerebrospinal fluid but also nerves and part of the spinal cord itself, which is usually deformed and open on the surface. Although the commonest site is the lumbar region, the lesion can occur at any point on the spine. As a result there is always some degree of flaccid paralysis (floppiness) below the damaged vertebrae.

All cases of myelomeningocele involve the spinal cord. As a result, the legs may be severely paralysed and congenital dislocation of the hip is common. As well as paralysis, many children have poor blood circulation and loss of skin sensation to pain, temperature, and touch. Burns and pressure sores can result without them being aware of it. When sitting or lying for long periods, it is important to change the position regularly to avoid undue pressure.

iii) *Anencephaly* In this condition, the brain does not develop properly and the baby is stillborn or dies shortly after birth.

More than 80% of babies born with spina bifida also have a condition called hydrocephalus (commonly known as 'water on the brain'), although this can occur quite independently. The condition is due to an abnormal accumulation of cerebrospinal fluid under pressure and, if untreated, can cause eventual brain damage and death. Congenital hydrocephalus is due mainly to malformations of the brain causing blockage to the flow of fluid and separation of the joints of the skull, resulting in enlargement of the skull. Acquired hydrocephalus may occur at any age as a result of head injuries, cerebral haemorrhage, or meningitis.

Causes/Inheritance pattern The precise cause of spina bifida is not known, but it is suggested that there are both hereditary and environmental factors involved. The risk for the general population as a whole with no family history is about 1 in 250. If there is a family history, the risk is about 1 in 25 for a second child being affected and 1 in 8 for a third. Thus it is not necessarily an inherited condition but, once a child with spina bifida has been born into a family, there is an increased risk of a subsequent child having a neural defect. Genetic counselling is available for parents who are known to be at risk.

Diagnosis/Treatment Thirty years or more ago, most babies born with spina bifida died shortly after birth from meningitis, infections, and hydrocephalus. Surgeons can now close the lesion on the back and prevent infection occuring. Since 1958, it has been possible to insert a shunt which drains off excess fluid from the brain and controls the hydrocephalus. Nevertheless, even with this operation, for some children there can be disturbances of vision, lack of concentration, and learning difficulties. However, since 1972 it has been possible to detect neural tube defects before birth with the use of amniocentesis, ultrasound, or scan.

Hydrocephalus requires early treatment if damage to the brain is to be avoided. Untreated hydrocephalus may lead to mental handicap and visual impairment. Early diagnosis is thus vital. For this reason, those babies at risk need to be observed carefully — particularly those of low birth weight or who have suffered birth trauma. Measurement of the head circumference of all babies is now routine, so that abnormal rate of growth can be more easily detected. It is sometimes considered that only those babies with a favourable prognosis should receive immediate surgery, but this is a decision for parents to make following full consultation and counselling.

Early support to parents is crucial, and the family should have the opportunity to discuss the nature of their child's condition with the medical specialist as well as with those in the community support services. Families need to feel that their child can participate in the usual activities for their age, for example, playgroups, day nurseries, etc.

Family living   Most children with severe spina bifida are incontinent and require some artificial form of control — such as catheterisation (insertion of a tube). This will enable the person to be freed from embarrassment and to take part in family and outside activities. Bladder and kidney infections are common and require treatment to prevent permanent damage.

Paralysis in the lower limbs results in muscle tensions becoming unbalanced, and bone deformities may occur. Some children may have brittle bones, and breaks may occur without the person being aware of it.

Hydrocephalus can produce squints and poor hand co-ordination. The latter limits writing, dressing, eating, etc. When a person experiences drowsiness, severe headache, and vomiting, it is essential to seek medical attention, as the shunting system which drains off excess fluid from the brain may be blocked.

For these reasons and others, children and young people with spina bifida may spend long periods in hospital. This can be particularly frustrating for young adults who are trying to establish themselves in the world and gain independence.

Young people need the contact of others of similar age and to participate in outside activities and leisure pursuits. Many people with spina bifida have married and proven their ability to cope.

For those who are more severely affected, day-care provision may be appropriate. Respite care offers a very essential break for families.

Education Children with spina bifida and/or hydrocephalus may experience a great many related problems. There are differences according to the type and degree of disability and in particular between children with and without hydrocephalus. Since the Education Act 1981, many more children with special needs are attending mainstream schools. However, due to related problems, some children may have severe or moderate learning difficulties and it may be more appropriate for them to attend a special school provided either by the local education authority or by a private or charitable organisation.

Those who have hydrocephalus may experience learning difficulties in relation to perceptual, motor co-ordination, and language skills. Children often have difficulty in judging position and movement in space. They can thus have problems in diagram work, extracting information from illustrations, judgement of size, etc. There may be hand—eye co-ordination difficulties and an inability to distinguish right from left.

Most children are verbally quite fluent, but do not necessarily show a corresponding comprehension of a subject. Concentration may be difficult, and attention on a one-to-one basis can be beneficial.

Frequent stays in hospital, lack of early stimulation in babyhood, sensory impairment, and emotional problems can all contribute to learning problems.

Employment For those more severely affected, attendance at a social-care centre, adult training centre, or sheltered workshop may be most appropriate, but there should be an emphasis on continuous assessment and training.

Other people will be able to find jobs and, with the use of specialist aids and equipment, keep in regular employment. Some undertake computer work.

Mobility/Aids and benefits Some children use calipers, and some need occasional or more frequent use of a wheelchair.

Attendance allowance and mobility allowance are usually appropriate, together with other benefits in relation to individual or family needs from the DHSS. Disability Alliance is one example of a specialist organisation which can advise on current benefits.

From an early age, children need to be encouraged to be as independent as possible. The range of aids can be discussed with the occupational therapist or the nearest disability advice centre. Alterations or adaptations to the family home may be appropriate. The social services department can assist in these areas.

Support agencies Advice on aids, appliances, education, mobility, employment and training, social welfare, independence training, etc.

can be obtained through the Association for Spina Bifida and Hydro-cephalus (ASBAH).

ASBAH has specialist officers as well as area fieldworkers. The orga-nisation runs a residential centre, called Five Oaks, which provides holi-days, independence training, and leisure courses.

The Spastics Society and the Royal Society for Mentally Handicapped Children and Adults (Mencap) can also provide support, literature, and guidance for those with hydrocephalus.

Useful literature

- *Children with spina bifida at school*, P. Henderson (ASBAH, 1975)
- *Young people with spina bifida and/or hydrocephalus: learning and development*, Leonie Holgate (ASBAH, 1986)
- *Sex and spina bifida* (ASBAH, 1985)
- *Further education and vocational training of young people with spina bifida and hydrocephalus*, Hazel Bonner (ASBAH, 1984)
- *Spina bifida and you*, Collette Welch (ASBAH, 1986)
- *The child with spina bifida*, Elizabeth M. Anderson and Bernie Spain (Methuen, 1977)
- *Disability in adolescence*, Elizabeth M. Anderson and Linda Clarke with Bernie Spain (Methuen, 1982)

Spinal-cord injury

Introduction   Damage to the spinal-cord nerves caused by the back or neck being broken in everyday accidents can result in paralysis. More rarely, disease (e.g. transverse myelitis) or loss of blood to the spinal nerves (e.g. when undergoing surgery) produces the same effect. Muscle power and sensation are lost or reduced from the point of the spinal-cord break (lesion) downwards.

Main characteristics   Paraplegia means paralysis of the lower limbs and part of the torso. Tetraplegia (sometimes known as quadriplegia) means paralysis of all four limbs, to varying degrees. Rarely only one limb is affected (monoplegia) or one side of the body (hemiplegia).

Diagnosis   Until proven otherwise by expert medical opinion supported by X-ray and other examination, a spinal injury needs to be regarded as potentially highly dangerous and likely to result in injury to the spinal cord, and paralysis, if inexpertly handled. Management designed to avoid this disaster therefore needs to begin at the site of the accident. During transport and attention by first-aiders, ambulance staff, etc., care should be taken not to flex, twist, or extend the spine.

During admission to hospital, vertebral-column damage may be aggravated due to the instability of the spinal column, and undue paralysis may result.

Treatment of spinal injuries requires specialist medical, nursing, and support staff. It is therefore crucial that people who are found to have sustained damage to their spinal column should be transferred immediately to a spinal-injury unit where possible.

Families of newly injured people need specialist information and support, and may welcome contact with others who share similar problems.

Treatment/Rehabilitation There are about twelve NHS spinal-injury units (SIUs) in the UK, and thus many people may have to receive treatment a long way from home. The biggest spinal-injuries unit is part of the Stoke Mandeville Hospital. SIUs are beginning to emphasise an interdisciplinary approach to care and treatment.

Some feel that there is too great an emphasis on physical care and that more attention should be given to the emotional impact of spinal injury. Adjusting to life in a wheelchair is a vital aspect of recovery.

Contact with an experienced wheelchair-user can help a newly disabled person overcome many of the practical problems of disability. Peer counselling, where there is no credibility gap if the counsellor is a wheelchair-user, can sometimes help to overcome feelings of shock and isolation. The Spinal Injuries Association (SIA) runs a 'Link' scheme that puts newly injured people in touch with experienced wheelchair-users for information and support. This service can also put the able-bodied relatives of a disabled person in touch with others who have experienced disability in the family for practical advice and support.

Due to the demanding care and attention required by very severely disabled people, it is not unusual for relatives and other carers to experience great problems in returning to a normal everyday life.

Many people — women in particular — find that the rehabilitation programmes do not always help them to cope with the double burden of working and running a home.

Complications not directly related to paralysis may occur, such as pressure sores, bladder and bowel problems, etc. Functional electrical stimulation of limbs and implants to operate the bladder are proving helpful in some cases.

Some people may experience spasms which may need control by drug therapy if they become too troublesome. Others experience persistent pain which in severe cases can be the most debilitating consequence of spinal-cord injury. Electrical stimulation of the spinal cord has been used to alleviate lower-limb spasticity and pain, but the results are variable.

Future treatment techniques may involve the more general use of drug therapy or electrical stimulation to aid nerve regrowth, 'cooling' techniques, 'hyperbaric oxygenation', and — perhaps one day — spinal-cord transplants. There has been a surge in research into reducing the degree of paralysis which will call for even more rapid admission to spinal units in the years to come.

Diet and exercise   Keeping fit is as important for a wheelchair-user as for able-bodied people. There may be a tendency to put on weight, and a well-balanced diet and regular exercise, if possible, are helpful. People who have high-lesion tetraplegia and who need to be lifted by carers may need to watch their weight carefully in order to avoid placing excessive strain on their helper.

Many people with tetraplegia — particularly lower-lesion tetraplegia — do achieve high levels of fitness, especially through swimming and other sporting activities.

Family living   The Spinal Injuries Association organises a care-attendant agency. This agency supplies experienced care attendants for short periods in the home or when a relative or other carer is away. It is seen as complementary and supplementary to existing care services.

The concept of 'integrated living' not only places an emphasis on people being independent in the sense of having their own place to live, where they have control over their physical help, but also requires that services should enable them to use transport, to work, to socialise, and to integrate into the mainstream of life.

For people who are more severely disabled, the choice between care in the community and residential care is an important example of decisions which people with a spinal injury must be allowed to make themselves. Appropriate support from the community agencies is necessary to enable more people to live independently at home, and people with a disability must have immediate control over how these services are provided in order that they have control over their own lives. People who are disabled must collectively have the major say in how services provided for their benefit are planned and operated.

Carers at home are rarely supported adequately and often need extra practical resources or, in some situations, the help of respite-care services.

Counselling concerning such areas as personal relationships and sex is vitally important, but unfortunately many units do not consider these aspects fully.

Incontinence is a major cause of embarrassment. Many feel that anxiety about incontinence would be lessened if access to decent toilet facilities away from home could be relied upon. Isolation is a problem particularly for women, who are encouraged to be dependent on others and not seek employment. This approach does not encourage a positive attitude towards rehabilitation.

Mobility   The choice of wheelchair is important and should in normal circumstances be made primarily by the person who is disabled. The person should be fully informed on the performance and special points of various types of wheelchair. Special consideration needs to be given to ensure that the wheelchair suits the person rather than vice versa. The wheelchair most widely used by people with spinal-cord injury is a standard E & J or Carter's model. Wheelchairs are obtainable from the DHSS and supplied by the local Artificial Limb and Appliance Centre (ALAC). Repairs and replacements are also undertaken by the ALAC. Lightweight new-generation wheelchairs and outdoor electric wheelchairs are currently not available from the DHSS, although the Manpower Services Commission may supply them for special work-related reasons.

The mobility allowance, together with one of the mobility schemes, can assist in financing the purchase or lease of a car adapted to the needs of a disabled driver or passenger.

Further education and training   Virtually all areas of study are suitable for people with a severe disability, although there are certain areas where a person might need to take an administrative or research post rather than a job in the field (although the SIA can give examples of people doing practical jobs in the field that would have been declared impossible by the professionals).

Computing offers many opportunities for those interested. Most levels of attainment can be accommodated, from data entry to the more technical jobs such as systems analysis. Many colleges and universities, including the Open University, offer computer training. The Queen Elizabeth College offers a residential computer-programming course for disabled people.

The National Bureau for Handicapped Students will be able to indicate which universities and colleges are able to accommodate wheelchair-users. Southampton and Sussex are examples of universities which are suitably equipped and have specially adapted halls of residence that will cater for all disabilities, including those experienced by students with very severe disability who need to employ carers.

Employment   Details of assessment and training centres, training courses, and rehabilitation units can be provided by the Employment Services Agency and the disablement resettlement officer. Various schemes aim to assist those who wish to work at home or who need specialist retraining or help with practical problems such as fares to work etc.

Aids and benefits   Aids centres can advise and give guidance concerning individual requirements. The Disabled Living Foundation offers a specialist service concerning aids. The Spinal Injuries Association also provides information on aids. Provision includes a suppository inserter as an aid to independence for people with tetraplegia.

Occupational-therapy units can offer guidance in the use of a whole range of aids. These include computers as aids to treatment and rehabilitation. Technological progress offers a variety of aids for use with a standard computer, and these are particularly useful to those with high-lesion tetraplegia. Speech synthesisers and electronic control systems increase the range of possibilities for computer use in rehabilitation.

Adaptations to the home may be an important requirement, and the social services department can usually assist.

The severe disablement allowance, introduced in 1984, is available for those people who cannot work because of long-term sickness or disablement and do not receive sickness benefit or invalidity benefit because they have not paid enough National Insurance contributions. Advice concerning the range of benefits available can be obtained from the DHSS or organisations such as citizens advice bureaux and the Disablement Income Group.

Support agencies   The Spinal Injuries Association acts as a central storehouse of information and expertise on spinal-cord injury. It is a self-help group whose aim is to assist people with paralysis and their families with the practical problems of reshaping their lives following injury.

A range of literature and a newsletter are available. An information service, a confidential welfare service, a personal-injury claims service, a 'Link' scheme, a relatives travel fund, and a care-attendant agency are provided. SIA holiday facilities include the first two narrowboats in the world designed to be controlled from a wheelchair.

The SIA pursues all matters of concern to people with spinal-cord injury at a local and national level. Together with other organisations, it actively works towards the full emancipation of people with a severe physical disability. At a practical level it actively works for proper access to education, employment, and 'the built environment' and towards the removal of all barriers to integration.

The SIA runs an information desk at the National Spinal Injuries Centre, Stoke Mandeville Hospital, and hopes to expand this service to other units.

Other relevant organisations include the Disabled Living Foundation, the British Council of Organisations of Disabled People, SEQUAL (Special Equipment and Aids for Living), the British Computer Society's specialist group for the disabled, the British Paraplegic Sports Society, PHAB (Physically Handicapped and Able Bodied), the Association of Carers, and Assistance and Independence for Disabled People (AID) (a commercial organisation to help people choose a car suited to them and to arrange finances).

Useful literature

- *So you're paralysed*, Bernadette Fallon (SIA, 1976)
- *Spinal-cord injuries: psychological, social and vocational adjustment*, Roberta Trieschmann (Pergamon, 1980)
- *Living with paraplegia*, Michael A. Rogers (Faber & Faber, 1986)
- *Help at hand: the who, how, where of caring* (Association of Carers, 1984)
- *Spinal injuries: guidance for general practitioners and district nurses*, Wyn Howarth (SIA, 1984)
- *Micros for handicapped users*, Peter Saunders (Helena Press, 1984)
- *Yoga for handicapped people*, Barbara Brosnan (Souvenir Press, 1982)
- *Fitness for the disabled: wheelchair users*, Jean Gairdner (Fitzhenry & Whiteside, 1983)
- *Aiming high: the story of Margaret Price*, David Hunn (Arthur Barker, 1984)
- *Social work with disabled people*, Michael Oliver (Macmillan, 1983)
- *Nursing management in the general hospital: the first 48 hours following injury* (SIA, 1980)
- *Tetraplegia and paraplegia*, Ida Bromley (Churchill Livingstone, 1981)

Stroke

Introduction   At least 100 000 people in the UK have a stroke for the first time each year. A stroke is a condition in which part of the brain is damaged, usually suddenly, either as a result of a brain blood vessel being blocked by a clot or due to a haemorrhage from a brain artery.

In many people the result is weakness or paralysis of the arm and leg on one side of the body; twisting of the face, and sometimes speech disturbance; difficulty with vision, swallowing, or balance; and loss of bladder control.

Even when paralysis is severe, there is often little effect on the intellect, although comprehension may be interfered with so that allowance needs to be made for a slowness to grasp new ideas.

Main characteristics   Strokes can produce a wide range of effects, depending on the region of the brain affected and the size of the blood vessel involved. At the onset of the stroke the muscles of the face, trunk, arm, and leg on either the left or the right side of the body may be weak and lax. Although the power gradually returns, first to the leg and then to the arm, it is crucial that great care is taken in handling the person concerned and that affected limbs are maintained in a position to allow maximum recovery.

Vision is not always affected but, when it is, it can be very disturbing. However, recovery usually occurs, albeit slowly.

Speech may be affected in one of two main ways:

i) Dysarthria is where articulation is impaired, usually due to the throat muscles being affected. Speech is slurred, indistinct, and sometimes absent altogether. However, the person can read and write and understand what is said. Dysarthria usually responds to treatment.

ii) Dysphasia or aphasia is where the part of the brain which controls language processes is damaged. This can affect the ability to speak, to understand speech, to read and write, etc. Almost half of those people whose right side of the body is paralysed are affected in this way. There are varying degrees of disability, and usually recovery is slow and incomplete — needing a great deal of support, understanding, and specialised help.

It is important to consider that the emotions may be more pronounced after a stroke — the person may laugh or cry more readily, and depression is a quite common result.

Causes   The cause is not known with certainty, but most strokes occur in later life and may be the result of damage to the blood vessels which has been building up slowly for several years.

Several factors are known to predispose towards a stroke, the main one being hypertension or raised blood pressure. Heart disease and diabetes are additional contributors. Both sexes are affected, and the use of the contraceptive pill by women may also be a factor.

Treatment   Partial recovery is usual, and the person adapts to the loss of function, although many are left with moderate or severe disability.

Admission to hospital is usual where skilled nursing, physiotherapy, occupational therapy, speech therapy, and involvement of the social worker from an early stage are important. Domiciliary services may be required when the person returns home, to maintain the rehabilitation process which may continue for months or even years at home.

Rehabilitation is very much part of the treatment process, and the favoured approach is to treat the person as a whole rather than concentrating on the affected arm or leg. This is done by working to a carefully devised pattern which may take anything from one to six months before sufficient skills, confidence, and security in walking can be achieved. The involvement of family or relatives in therapy sessions before discharge from hospital is often encouraged.

In order to reduce the risk of a stroke or a recurrence — particularly for those who have coronary heart disease or another cardiac condition — it is crucial to eliminate certain factors known to increase this risk. These factors are high blood pressure, cigarette smoking, high blood cholesterol (due mainly to animal fats in the diet), being overweight, and inactivity.

Family living To both the person affected by a stroke and his or her family, the slow rehabilitative period can be fraught with frustrations, aggression, and apathy. Stroke clubs and related support groups can be important in helping to relieve tension and enable people to share the day-to-day difficulties with others. It is often important for carers to have a break, and thus respite care may need to be arranged at regular intervals. Local facilities for this provision may be limited, however.

It is important to allow the person to be as independent as possible, despite the degree of handicap and the time taken to manage self-care, although it is often very difficult for family members not to try to assist. Much progress in improvement of use of the affected part can occur with perseverance of therapy.

One major concern that the family may experience is the fear of a further stroke, but this is not very common.

As strokes generally occur from middle age, the disability may bring serious changes to the lives of the family members — particularly in terms of employment expectations, leisure activities, and changed individual responsibilities.

Further training/Employment Few people of working age are able to return to their original occupation after a stroke. Retraining can be offered in specialised centres or through the Department of Employment.

Aids and benefits Some people may find that they cannot return to employment, and long-term social-security schemes may be needed. Mobility allowance, attendance allowance, and invalid care allowance may be appropriate.

Adaptations to the home may be necessary, together with equipment to make life easier for the disabled person, and can be arranged through the rehabilitation officer or occupational therapist within the social services department.

Support agencies The hospital team, family doctor, community nurse, social-services-department social worker, and occupational therapist are all important sources of support and information. In addition the Chest, Heart and Stroke Association (CHSA) provides helpful literature for families and can give information concerning local support groups etc. In addition to counselling and welfare services, the CHSA organises volunteer stroke schemes in which volunteers visit those with speech problems at home. There is also a national network of stroke clubs providing support to those with or without speech problems.

The British Heart Foundation will also provide useful information and guidance.

Useful literature

- *A time to speak*, Valerie Eaton Griffith, Patricia Oetliker, and Prue Oswin (CHSA, 1983)
- *Help yourself: a handbook for hemiplegics and their families*, Peggy Jay (Ian Henry Publications, 4th edition 1985)
- *Stroke: the facts*, F. Clifford Rose (Oxford University Press, 1981)
- *Return to mobility: exercises for stroke patients*, Margaret Hawker and Amanda Squires (CHSA, 2nd edition 1985)
- *Recovering from a stroke*, Heart Research Series, No. 3 (British Heart Foundation)
- *Feeling better? — Stroke*, Maeve Robertson (Channel Four Television, 1981)

The CHSA also provides an extensive range of booklets.

Tuberous sclerosis

Introduction Tuberous sclerosis (TS) is a rare hereditary condition. Its incidence is approximately 1 in 10 000 in the UK.

In general, tuberous sclerosis is not progressive or degenerative as such, but some people may experience complications or side-effects as a result of treatment to control the main symptoms.

The condition takes its name from the sclerotic (hardened) tuber-shaped areas which calcify in the brain. These lesions can be found anywhere in the brain and tend to grow slowly.

TUBEROUS SCLEROSIS
THE GENETIC INHERITANCE PATTERN

ONE PARENT HAS T S

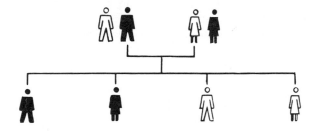

ONE IN TWO CHANCE OF CHILD DEVELOPING T S

UNAFFECTED

TUBEROUS
SCLEROSIS

Inheritance pattern In many cases (about 50%) the altered gene for TS appears by mutation, and thus only the child is affected. Sometimes TS is inherited but it may have been so mild in the parent that it had not been detected. A person with TS can pass on the condition, as it is dominantly inherited, and there is thus a 1 in 2 chance of passing on the condition. It is preferable that all children in the family are tested for TS once diagnosis has been made.

The involvement of the genetic counsellor is an important part of management of the condition.

Diagnosis/Treatment The earliest signs may be patches of white skin, especially on the limbs and body, which can sometimes be seen from birth. In about 70% of cases, a characteristic facial rash (butterfly rash) appears across the nose and cheeks as the child grows. The rash can sometimes be effectively treated by a dermatologist.

A brain scan can sometimes confirm diagnosis of TS.

There is a tendency (80%) for children with TS to develop epilepsy. Infantile spasms are common, and as the child gets older the type of seizure changes. Autistic behaviour may also be present. Control with the use of anticonvulsant drugs is important.

Many people with TS have average intelligence, but some children do begin to show a slowness in learning once the seizures start. About 60% experience mental handicap, which can be intensified by the epileptic seizures. Regular assessment is an important feature of treatment.

Speech and communication are particular areas where help may be needed.

Family living The problems of epilepsy and mental handicap can be particularly stressful where there are additional behavioural disturbances. Anxiety may be increased by the guilt experienced by a parent who realises that he or she has passed on the condition. Early support to families is thus crucial.

Long-term care may become necessary, but short-term breaks and holiday provision are valuable. Parents are often concerned by the long-term question of care when they are no longer able to provide their child with support. Social services departments can usefully be involved at an early stage to provide support and counselling to families before crises develop.

Education Home teachers, playgroups, toy libraries, speech therapy, and physiotherapy can all help children to achieve their full potential. Some children will be more appropriately taught in schools for children with special needs.

Drug therapy, used to control seizures, frequently interferes with learning and may affect behaviour.

Employment Through the assistance of the disablement resettlement officer, provision of sheltered employment can be arranged where appropriate. The type of employment is clearly related to the severity of TS. Many may attend their local adult training centre.

Aids and benefits For the most severely handicapped, home adaptations may become necessary and can be arranged through the social services departments.

Attendance allowance and mobility allowance may be appropriate. Families should seek advice on which DHSS benefits are relevant to their situation.

Support agencies The Tuberous Sclerosis Association was set up in 1977 and hopes to promote a better understanding of TS. Literature and a newsletter are available. National and local meetings are held, and a contact scheme is offered.

The Disabled Living Foundation and the Royal Society for Mentally Handicapped Children and Adults (Mencap) can also provide advice and assistance.

Useful literature

- *When bad things happen to good people*, W. Harold and S. Kushner (Pan, 1982)
- *People with epilepsy: how to help them*, Mary and John Laidlaw (Churchill Livingstone, 1984)
- *Childhood incontinence*, Roger Morgan (Disabled Living Foundation, 1984)
- *After I'm gone: what will happen to my handicapped child?*, Gerald Sanctuary (Souvenir Press, 1984)
- *Getting through to your handicapped child*, Elizabeth Newson and Tony Hipgrave (Cambridge University Press, 1982)

Neuro-muscular disorders

Motor neurone disease

Introduction Motor neurone disease (MND) is the name given to a group of related diseases affecting the motor neurones in the brain and spinal cord. These nerve cells controlling the muscles are slowly destroyed, which may result in progressive weakness and paralysis. Such wasting is due to the nerve supply being cut off and generally occurs in the arms and legs, although some groups of muscles are more affected than others.

MND is generally progressive over a variable period of time, but in rare cases the progression may halt temporarily.

The average course of the disease is between three and five years, but some people have lived for 10 to 20 years following onset.

Men are affected twice as often as women.

MND occurs in countries all over the world, with about the same percentage of the population being affected. However, an abnormally high rate was evident in a few small areas in the world, including the Western Pacific island of Guam, Western New Guinea, and the Japanese Kii peninsula.

One in 50 000 people will develop MND per year, and there are 5000 cases in the UK. The onset is usually in late middle age, mostly at over 40 years, although there have been cases as young as 20 years.

There are three main types of MND, of which amyotrophic lateral sclerosis (ALS) is the most common. The other two types are progressive muscular atrophy and progressive bulbar palsy, but there is considerable overlap between all three clinical categories.

Main characteristics MND does not affect the senses, nor bladder or bowel control directly. The intellect remains unchanged.

Early symptoms include cramps in affected muscles, general fatigue, and twitching (fasciculations). All of these become worse after exercise.

62

Spasticity (stiffness) and jerking of the arms and legs may also be experienced, although some people may develop flaccidity (floppiness) or a mixture of spasticity and flaccidity. Weakness usually starts in the hands and feet, with some muscles being affected more than others. This weakness worsens with time. Some people with a particular type of MND may develop 'bulbar' or 'pseudobulbar' symptoms, which means that the muscles important for production of speech and swallowing may be affected. When this occurs, weakness and wasting in the muscles of the face and throat lead to swallowing, chewing, and speech difficulties. Speech can be slurred, nasal, and have a monotonous tone.

Causes   There is no known cause of MND, but some past theories suggested links with viral infection, heavy-metal poisoning, metabolic disturbances, and immunological defects. It is not contagious.

Inheritance pattern   There is no hereditary pattern for the great majority of families. In a small percentage (5 to 10%) of cases there appears to be a familial pattern, with more than one member of the family being affected.

Diagnosis   In the early stages the symptoms may be slight. Thus the condition may have been present for some time before diagnosis or the onset of main symptoms. Due largely to the variable nature of the condition, an incorrect diagnosis may be made in the early stages.

The neurologist may use various diagnostic tests on an in-patient or out-patient basis. These include an electromyogram (EMG), which involves testing the electrical activity of the muscles; a myelogram (introduction of a dye into the spinal cord); and sometimes a lumbar puncture, a procedure used to take a sample of fluid from the spinal cord. Tests may need to be repeated at intervals of a few months in order to make a definite diagnosis.

Treatment   There is no specific treatment to arrest or slow down the progress of this condition. Some symptoms can be effectively alleviated by the combined use of drugs, physical aids, physiotherapy, and speech therapy.

Both the hospital consultant and the family doctor are important sources of support and information, together with the nurse, physiotherapist, speech therapist, dietician, social worker, and occupational therapist. However, the family doctor may have little knowledge of MND and so may be unable to offer help in the most effective way. The average family doctor may see only one case in nine years.

Diet and exercise   As approximately 50% of those with MND find difficulty in chewing food and 75% have some problems with swallowing, the choice of food needs consideration. Various aids and drugs can alleviate these problems. A balance needs to be achieved between continuing use of muscles and avoiding over-use which causes acute fatigue.

Family living   The family often feel shocked and disbelieving following diagnosis. In addition the person with MND has to cope with the frustrations of the condition — progressive wasting in the body, yet with the intellect remaining unaffected. Continued independence is important in maintaining self-esteem and dignity.

Those people who have a speech difficulty in particular may find that children are embarrassed and neighbours and friends may not understand and, due to lack of knowledge, assume the person to be mentally ill or brain-damaged.

It is thought to be most supportive where families are fully informed of the diagnosis and its meaning, with follow-up help and information being available. Families can then organise their lives to maintain, as much as possible, a normal lifestyle. Many people manage to live full and productive lives even when the condition is quite far advanced. This is usually easier where speech is less affected.

Anger, isolation, and frustration are understandable reactions in adjusting to the changing condition, and periods of hospitalisation can be disheartening. Depression is also a natural reaction, and the family doctor or social worker may be an appropriate source of support.

Some people experience a loss of voluntary control over their emotions so that laughing or crying may suddenly occur inappropriately, which can be distressing to the individual and the family. It is very important that these symptoms are understood to be part of the physical condition.

Pain and discomfort may, for some, make sleeping difficult, and guidance from the physiotherapist can be helpful. The use of painkillers may be necessary.

Many people with MND have no use of their legs and arms, and experience additional bulbar difficulties (such as impaired swallowing ability). This provides a full range of handicap and leads to serious disability.

Residential and/or nursing care may be required in the later stages of the condition. This disorder is terminal, and continuing support to the individual and the family is therefore crucial.

Mobility   Because of leg and trunk weakness, some people may eventually require a wheelchair and become completely immobile.

Employment   In general, continued employment is encouraged for as long as reasonably possible, and various aids such as speech aids, computing aids, writing aids, etc. can assist.

Aids and benefits   The use of a variety of physical aids is important if a reasonable level of independence is to be maintained. These may include car adaptations, walking frames, crutches, stairlifts, adjustable beds, reclining chairs, wheelchairs, communication aids, etc. Adaptations within the home are often needed.

Appropriate benefits include the mobility allowance and attendance allowance.

Support agencies   Several organisations are important in assisting people and their families to obtain a satisfactory level of independence in all respects. Some of these are the Disabled Living Foundation, Motability, the Association of Carers, Voluntary Organisations Communication and Language (VOCAL), and the Muscular Dystrophy Group of Great Britain and Northern Ireland.

The hospital team and the local social services department are important sources of support and information.

The Motor Neurone Disease Association provides useful literature on symptoms and management for families and professionals. A regular newsletter and branches across the UK offer guidance and assistance in addition to the Association's patient-care officers, who give specialist advice and counselling and arrange a voluntary visiting scheme. The MNDA has a small amount of equipment available for free loan and also raises funds for research projects.

Useful literature

- *Plain man's guide to MND*, J.R. Tew (MNDA)
- 'Multiple sclerosis and motor neurone disease', M. Holbrook and P. Alsop (*Social work service*, vol. 27, pp. 41–5, September 1981)
- 'Motor neurone disease', V. Rose (*Journal of district nursing*, August 1982, pp. 4–7)
- *Hospice: the living idea*, ed. C. Saunders, D.H. Summers, and N. Teller (Edward Arnold, 1981) (See the chapter 'Hospice care in motor neurone disease: a review of 100 cases'.)
- 'Must not despair', C. Cox (*Nursing mirror*, 21 October 1981, pp. 44–7)

Muscular dystrophy

Introduction   There are several hundred different disorders which may affect the muscles and the nerve supply to the muscles. Information concerning myasthenia gravis and motor neurone disease is given separately. Spinal muscular atrophy and myotonia congenita are discussed at the end of this chapter.

Of the disorders which affect muscle fibres, the main group is the muscular dystrophies. There are several different kinds, all of which are progressive, hereditary, and result in muscle weakness.

The slow, progressive breakdown of the muscle fibres over several years leads to the destruction of the muscle tissue. During this time, the damaged fibres attempt to regenerate but are replaced by fibrous tissue and fat. The resulting muscle weakness and loss of muscle bulk cause difficulty in walking and in the use of the arms and may eventually become severely disabling.

The main types of muscular dystrophy affecting children and adults are the Duchenne type, the Becker type, scapulohumeral and scapuloperoneal (formerly known as 'limb girdle') types, the facioscapulohumeral type, and myotonic dystrophy. Rarer types include congenital, ocular, and distal muscular distrophies and the 'autosomal recessive' childhood form. In general, different types are classified according to the muscle groups involved.

Main characteristics/Inheritance pattern

Duchenne type   This is the most common form of muscular dystrophy and, in general, the most severe. With very rare exceptions it affects boys only and is inherited in the female line. Mothers, sisters, and other female relatives may be 'carriers' of the inheritance factor and may thus pass on the condition to their sons. Tests can confirm diagnosis, but there is no cure.

At birth there is no apparent disability and it is not usually until the age of two to five years that clumsiness in walking, frequent falls, and some difficulty in running become evident. Later there is increasing difficulty in running, in climbing stairs, and in standing up after a fall.

The muscle weakness is slowly progressive so that, by the age of about 9 to 11 years, the boy becomes unable to walk and will need the assistance of a wheelchair. Everyday activities become more difficult as the arms become weaker.

Prevention by identification of carriers and genetic counselling is an important aspect of management and care.

Exercise is very important in maintaining muscle strength for as long as possible, and thus physiotherapy is vital.

Certain muscles are affected initially, and others follow as the condition progresses. Weakness of the back muscles may result in curvature of the spine. Eventually the muscles of the face, hands, and of respiration are affected and the boy's life is at risk. At around 16 to 25 years of age, respiratory infections usually prove fatal.

Becker type   This is less common than Duchenne dystrophy, but the same muscles are involved; however, the condition is milder. Diagnosis is usually made at some time between late childhood and the twenties. Progression is slow, and the person may often be able to walk until his thirties or middle age. Thus it is possible to maintain a full working life, although at some stage the person will become wheelchair-bound.

As with Duchenne type, only boys are affected. An affected boy's sisters have a 1 in 2 chance of carrying the genetic factor, and all his daughters will be carriers but his sons will be unaffected.

Scapulohumeral type   This disorder is not very common. It affects the shoulder muscles and later the thigh muscles. Diagnosis is usually made in early adulthood, and progression is slow.

Both sexes are affected, and there is a 1 in 4 risk that subsequent brothers or sisters will be affected. Inheritance is recessive. Unless the person marries a close relative, the chances of children being affected are low.

Scapuloperoneal type   This is a fairly uncommon condition which affects mainly the shoulder and leg muscles. Inheritance may be similar to that of the Duchenne type or dominant like the facioscapulohumeral type.

Facioscapulohumeral type   This type is generally mild, but severity can be very variable. For some people, disability may be evident in their twenties, but for others diagnosis may not occur until old age.

Face and shoulder muscles are usually the most severely affected, and initial signs may appear before the age of 20 years.

Inheritance is dominant, which means that each person with this type of dystrophy has one or the other parent affected and that children of an affected parent have a 1 in 2 chance of being affected themselves.

Myotonic dystrophy   This conditions occurs more in adults than in children. It affects other parts of the body in addition to muscles — such as the eye, the heart, and sometimes the nervous system. Together with muscle weakness, there is a difficulty in relaxing muscles (myotonia). The latter is usually evident first but can be alleviated with certain drugs. Symptoms may develop before the age of 10 years, and diagnosis is usually reached by 25 years. Children may find speech difficult, due to the myotonia, and thus may benefit from speech therapy.

Only a few people find that the severity of muscle weakness requires a wheelchair before their fifties. However, the additional symptoms, together with a slow deterioration in physical and mental energy, can result in a seriously disabling condition.

The inheritance is dominant, and therefore children of an affected

MUSCULAR DYSTROPHY
DUCHENNE AND BECKER TYPES
THE GENETIC INHERITANCE PATTERN

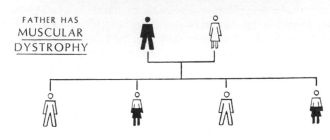

FATHER HAS
MUSCULAR
DYSTROPHY

ALL DAUGHTERS ARE CARRIERS

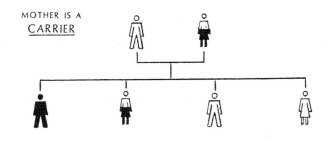

MOTHER IS A
CARRIER

ONE IN TWO CHANCE OF SON HAVING MUSCULAR DYSTROPHY
ONE IN TWO CHANCE OF DAUGHTER BEING A CARRIER

 UNAFFECTED   CARRIER    MUSCULAR DYSTROPHY

MUSCULAR DYSTROPHY
FACIOSCAPULOHUMERAL & MYOTONIC TYPES
THE GENETIC INHERITANCE PATTERN

ONE PARENT HAS M D

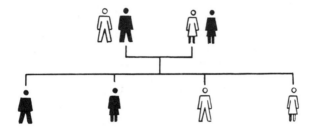

ONE IN TWO CHANCE OF CHILD DEVELOPING M D

UNAFFECTED

MUSCULAR
DYSTROPHY

parent have a 1 in 2 chance of developing the condition.

Diagnosis/Treatment   Childhood muscular dystrophy is usually diagnosed as mobility problems become evident. Other types are not apparent until later life. However, for Duchenne and Becker types, where there is a family history, diagnosis can be made through a blood test well before symptoms appear.

Parents frequently realise that there is something wrong long before diagnosis can be reached. This can be a very frustrating time, particularly when delay in walking is attributed initially to other factors. Once muscular dystrophy is suspected, assessment is necessary through a specialist at a hospital centre. In addition to blood tests, diagnosis can be aided by an electromyogram (EMG), which examines the electrical activity of muscles, and a muscle biopsy (examination of a sample of muscle).

Parents and families need to be given as much information and support as possible, particularly in the early stages. Some hospital centres will offer comprehensive care where all members of the family become well known to the care team and support concerning medical, social, educational, and emotional matters is provided on a continuing basis.

The question of how much to tell a child with a progressive disorder is difficult for professionals as well as for parents. However, it is usually helpful for the child to be given opportunities to discuss his or her feelings away from the parents.

Physiotherapy and genetic counselling are vital elements of the treatment process.

Diet and exercise   People with muscular dystrophy tend to become overweight, especially when they are unable to walk. A well balanced diet is vital, and the hospital dietician can advise where necessary.

Exercise, particularly in relation to specialised physiotherapy, is of crucial importance to maintain overall health and self-respect. There is no shortage of organisations concerned with sport, leisure, and outdoor pursuits nationwide.

Family living   Families naturally experience grief once diagnosis is made and may have found the years and months leading up to confirmation traumatic. Parents may find the inheritance implications too distressing to comprehend, and feelings of guilt on the part of the parent who is the 'carrier' may cause tension within the family.

There may be another child in the family likely to be affected, which creates additional stress. Shielding the child from the reality of the future and not allowing full independence similar to other children of the same age may lead to difficult behaviour in adolescence. Sharing feelings and difficulties with other families and making use of professional help are valuable aspects of support.

Parents may find that they feel embarrassed in public and avoid such situations — feelings which can be passed on to the child. The need for privacy and independence will lead to additional frustrations for the young person. The need for permanent care can equally be distressing to parents, but practical support helps relieve the depression or anxiety often felt. Families may sometimes feel that respite care, alternative carers, and assistance with holidays are more important than some professionals realise.

Some local authorities provide sheltered housing or domiciliary services so that a person with a disability can live as independently as possible and take full advantage of the facilities within the community. Voluntary organisations, local authorities, and private concerns may offer residential homes. Social services departments keep a list of such facilities in their local areas or nearby. It is helpful to visit homes well in advance, in order to make a realistic decision concerning the most appropriate type of accommodation and for families to adjust to this change. Many residential homes have long waiting lists.

Mobility Most forms of muscular dystrophy affect mobility to a greater or lesser extent. The self-respect which independence gives in this and other areas should not be underestimated.

Through the mobility-allowance scheme, available to those between 5 and 66 years who satisfy the criteria, it is possible to join car-purchase schemes and arrange adaptations.

Education In the early stages of this condition, children frequently attend their local nursery, playgroup, and primary school. For a few children it may become apparent that special provision is more beneficial. However this can be frustrating to families if this decision is made only on practical grounds, without considering the emotional welfare of the child.

With the current emphasis on vocational, functional, and social integration, notably following the Education Act 1981, the number of children with severe disabilities attending mainstream schools has acceptably increased. Full assessment of each child should be made with the involvement of parents, professionals, and teaching staff so that the most appropriate placement can be recommended, whether this be a mainstream school, a school for children with special needs, or a residential school. Practical problems may prevent a child who is wheelchair-bound from attending a mainstream school.

A child and his or her family need to understand the reasons for a change of school, so that a feeling of failure is not felt. For boys who have Duchenne muscular dystrophy there may be some intellectual limitations involving memory and verbal fluency. However, approximately half of those affected fall within the average range of intelligence and might be expected to cope academically in a mainstream school. The intellectual limitation is not progressive.

Leaving school can be a particularly traumatic period, especially for the boy with Duchenne who will be aware of his physical condition rapidly declining.

Further education and training   Opportunities within particular career fields and school attainment are important factors when further training is considered. Support, guidance, and assessment are vital during the latter school years in identifying realistic career choices with the assistance of the school staff, careers officer, school medical officer, and disablement resettlement officer.

Courses at college can be difficult to arrange where heavy dependence on others for toileting and minor nursing is necessary.

A number of specialised residential colleges of further education provide assessment and courses often adapted to meet individual needs.

Employment   Employment possibilities may be hindered by lack of assessment and likewise understanding by all concerned of the true potential or capabilities of each person. It is important to encourage participation in training and employment rather than make decisions in consideration of the likely future deterioration and disablement.

Most people who are disabled are registered with the social services department so that provision of the necessary special facilities can be considered. Some, however, also choose to register with the Department of Employment once they reach 16 years of age.

Sheltered employment or work at home may be more suitable.

The growth of employment in the field of computers has been advantageous in both open and home-based employment.

Aids and benefits.   To those with muscular dystrophy, everyday activities of life prove the most difficult, and thus it is important that aids are made appropriate to each individual person. Information concerning aids and adaptations to the home can be found through aids centres and through the social worker and occupational therapist working within the social services department. Occasionally it may be advisable to attend an assessment centre for comprehensive guidance and rehabilitation.

Advice and information concerning available benefits can be found through the DHSS, social services departments, and the Disablement Income Group. Those that are usually relevant include mobility allowance, attendance allowance, invalid care allowance, invalidity benefit, improvement grants, etc. Benefit schemes are being constantly revised, so families should be encouraged to find out what is available through the relevant organisations.

Support agencies In addition to the statutory departments, a range of voluntary organisations can provide useful information and guidance to families. These include the Disabled Living Foundation, the Invalid Children's Aid Association, the Disablement Income Group, and the Royal Association for Disability and Rehabilitation (RADAR).

The Muscular Dystrophy Group of Great Britain and Northern Ireland provides comprehensive support and regularly updated information to families and carers. A patient-care department is based at their head office, and family-care officers are based at some of the main neuro-muscular centres throughout the country. In addition, there is a network of local support groups.

Useful literature

From the Muscular Dystrophy Group of Great Britain and Northern Ireland:

● *With a little help*, Philippa Harpin (1981)
● *The muscular dystrophy handbook* (a practical guide for those who suffer from muscular dystrophy and allied neuro-muscular diseases)
● *Opportunities in micro-electronics for disabled people* (1982)

Spinal muscular atrophy

This condition may closely resemble muscular dystrophy and may cause similar problems. It is a disorder of the motor neurones, and muscles become weak because of the loss of some of the nerve cells in the spinal cord which control muscle contraction.

This disorder ranges from a severe progressive deterioration in babies of under a year (which is usually fatal) to a much milder disorder of late childhood and adult life (Kugelberg—Welander disease).

Inheritance is variable, but there is a risk that brothers or sisters may be affected.

Milder cases have long periods where the condition does not deteriorate, and even quite severe disability in early infancy may not show deterioration for several years. Most people do eventually require a wheelchair, however.

Exercises, together with prevention of joint and spinal deformities, are helpful but there is no known cure.

The Muscular Dystrophy Group of Great Britain and Northern Ireland can provide additional information and support.

Myotonia congenita (Thomsen's disease)

This is a comparatively rare inherited disorder. It is characterised by an inability to relax the muscles following forceful contraction. The other features of myotonic dystrophy are absent, and there is no atrophy (wasting) of the muscles.

Onset is usually at between three to six years of age, and the child starts to walk hesitatingly but then with a more normal gait. Sustained muscle contractions may last for up to 30 seconds, and usually the legs are affected.

The myotonia may be partially relieved by the use of certain drugs, and physiotherapy is helpful.

Prognosis can be varied. In milder cases, limiting factors may not provide major difficulties in living a near to normal life, but in severe cases the child may be wheelchair-bound.

In families where the symptoms start in infancy the inheritance is dominant, often passing through many generations. When the onset is later, the inheritance is usually recessive.

Further information and support can be obtained from the Muscular Dystrophy Group of Great Britain and Northern Ireland.

Myasthenia gravis

Introduction   Myasthenia gravis (MG) means 'serious muscle weakness'.

It is a neuro-muscular disorder in which there is a defect in the action of the chemical substance (acetylcholine) which transmits messages across nerve−muscle junctions. MG is characterised by varying weakness of the voluntary muscles of the body, i.e. those muscles which perform intentional actions. This weakness is abnormally increased by continued or repeated use of the muscles at any one time, and strength is partially retrieved by short rest periods.

The incidence is about 1 in 20 000 in the UK. As a result of progress in research and treatment, the outlook for people with MG is now very much improved.

Main characteristics   Weakness is the most frequent characteristic of this disorder and it is greatest after exercise. Those muscles which are often affected in the early stages are related to vision, speech, chewing, and swallowing. The voice tends to become nasal and during conversation may become almost unintelligible. In later stages the arm and leg muscles weaken abnormally, causing difficulty in raising an arm and in walking etc. Some difficulty in breathing may be experienced. Additional symptoms which frequently occur include drooping eyelids, double vision, and general fatigue. Not all these symptoms are apparent for everyone, and the severity may vary from day to day. However the condition is noticeably worse as the day progresses, but improves with rest. Although this disorder is not common in children, it probably occurs more often than realised. A diagnosis as early as three months old has been known.

Causes MG has now been proven to be an auto-immune disease — the body, which usually manufactures antibodies to combat particular foreign substances in it, starts to manufacture antibodies which attack the body itself. In this case, the body becomes sensitive to the cells ('endplate receptors') which trigger muscular action when the nerve ending releases acetylcholine at a nerve — muscle junction. Under the control of the thymus gland, antibodies are manufactured which attack these cells and so interfere with the transmission of messages from nerve to muscle, causing muscle weakness.

MG occurs at all ages, but in most cases onset is at about 20 years. There is a secondary peak for men between 50 to 60 years. Before this age, women with the condition outnumber men by 4 to 1, but in late life men predominate.

Diagnosis Symptoms may be so slight in the early stages and deterioration so gradual that the disorder may not be quickly diagnosed. An injection of Tensilon is usually used to aid diagnosis of MG and may also be used in management.

An initial movement is performed normally but, on repeating it, muscles rapidly weaken and the movement becomes impossible. Strength recovers after rest. The muscles supplied by the cranial nerves are most commonly involved, then the neck muscles and the muscles used in respiration. Later the limbs are affected.

There are few hospitals which specialise in MG, and thus many families have to travel long distances for specialist advice and treatment.

When the distribution of muscle weakness is atypical, a misdiagnosis of psychiatric disease is not uncommon. For example, with an inability to smile and a frozen expression due to weak facial muscles, some people have been diagnosed as suffering from depression.

Treatment Routine treatment ('maintenance therapy') is usually required for life, but spontaneous recovery sometimes occurs. Drugs can control MG for some and may restore some measure of muscular strength for others. Without continued treatment, the condition usually becomes progressively more severe. Myasthenia responds to drugs ('cholinesterase inhibitors'), and regular treatment throughout the day (often four-hourly) by tablet or injection helps restore muscle strength. However medication needs regular adjustment, as too much will also hasten the progress of the muscle weakness.

Surgical removal of the thymus gland (thymectomy) appears to provide complete remission or a substantial improvement in about 80% of cases. It is not so helpful for those with the ocular type of MG (affecting only the eyes).

Improvement in treatment now means that many older people who were wheelchair-bound have been able to regain some muscle strength and movement.

Physiotherapy is not usually appropriate. Speech therapy is useful only in some cases.

With the establishment of MG as an auto-immune disease, new therapies to depress the manufacture of antibodies are being employed. Steroids and immunosuppressant drugs are now frequently used.

Diet and exercise   It is important to eat a nourishing, well balanced diet. Small meals at regular intervals are preferable to large amounts of food at one time.

Many people find that a warm drink and a biscuit or snack taken with the medication is helpful.

It is important not to smoke or drink alcohol — or to indulge only in moderation if either cannot be given up.

A compromise needs to be reached between keeping up a healthy amount of movement and excessive exercise. This can be especially difficult for children, who may not be able to run or participate in a wide range of play activities.

Family living   It is very necessary to make changes in lifestyle so that everything can be done at a moderate pace and periods of rest become part of the daily routine. Clearly for someone with blurred and double vision and difficulty in talking, chewing, swallowing, and maintaining continued movement of arms and legs, these are major handicaps. The frustrations become more acute as the condition worsens. For example, it is difficult or impossible to complete simple tasks such as brushing one's hair or shaving, as the muscles become too weak. Half-way through a meal, a person with MG may become unable to chew any longer. The implications that this disability has for every member of the family are thus chronic.

People with MG experience a great deal of mental and physical strain, and everyday activities are dependent on taking medication. It is often difficult to resist the temptation to increase medication. To remain smart and well groomed can sometimes seem too demanding, and yet a positive attitude is crucial to the person with the condition and his or her family.

MG is not brought about by psychosis or neurosis, but emotional stress commonly aggravates the condition. Infections such as colds will also aggravate MG, and thus it is important to take additional rest at these times. Many people find that extremes of temperature can produce adverse effects.

Mobility With the improved treatment, many older people who were wheelchair-bound are becoming more mobile. However stairs, steps, and long walking distances can be a problem if they need to be coped with regularly.

Some form of transport is undoubtedly very important if the person is to participate in life.

Education Children attend mainstream schools, but most are unable to participate in games. The ocular type of MG is significantly milder, and those with this condition can usually participate more fully in activities.

Employment Many find and keep in regular employment on a part-time or full-time basis. However, the choice of employment can be limited, and some people are not able to work because the right kind of sedentary job is not available.

Aids and benefits Adaptations to the home such as lifts, ramps, hand-rails, etc. are usually required. The use of labour-saving devices in the home is helpful, but it is necessary to assess the value of each aid on an individual basis.

A Lundie loop can provide a comfortable and unobtrusive prop for those whose eyelids tend to droop completely. The loop is attached to a pair of spectacles.

The severe disablement allowance, attendance allowance, and mobility allowance are the kinds of benefit frequently appropriate.

Support agencies The British Association of Myasthenics (BAM) was formed in the 1960s as a support and self-help group. It has close links with the Muscular Dystrophy Group of Great Britain and Northern Ireland. The Association has several chapters in various parts of the country, and great emphasis is placed on personal support.

Useful literature

BAM publishes a useful booklet entitled *The myasthenia gravis companion* and can provide additional information on request.

Poliomyelitis

Introduction   Poliomyelitis is a virus infection which starts with an acute illness lasting up to six weeks. A severe attack causes varying amounts of damage to the part of the brain and spinal cord responsible for the control of voluntary movement. This results in paralysis of muscles, which no longer receive any nerve impulse.

The degree of paralysis varies from one person to another. Some may require a respirator or be wheelchair-bound; others may be affected in only one limb, for example.

Main characteristics   Polio damages cells which control muscles. The muscle fibres are not affected, but they degenerate when they no longer receive a nervous stimulus and they are eventually replaced by fibrous tissue. After an attack of polio, residual paralysis is determined by the site and extent of damage to nerve cells. A muscle will be weakened if only a proportion of its controlling cells have died, but muscles will be lost and limbs made useless if brain-cell damage is extensive.

Secondary factors which may cause difficulties and physical disability include the following:

- Contracture (which produces a shrinking and shortening of the muscle) due to the unequal pull of opposing muscle groups and distortion of the trunk muscles caused by paralysis of the postural muscles.
- Lack of or unequal growth because of poor circulation in paralysed limbs, particularly when polio is contracted in childhood.
- Swelling and sensitivity to cold, due to poor circulation.
- Arthritis may occur in weight-bearing joints. Wrists, elbows, and shoulder joints may become worn largely as a result of strain from the use of walking aids.

Causes   Polio is thought to be passed on by contact with someone who has the disease or by a carrier (a person who does not have the disease but can transmit it). It is suggested also that it may be contracted by drinking water infected by the virus.

Polio has not been eradicated from the world and thus there is always a possibility of another outbreak. Protection by vaccine is vital. Approximately 84% of the child population in the UK is immunised.

Diagnosis/Treatment   The initial illness is followed by a long recovery period when a pattern of paralysis becomes established. Within one to seven days, fever, headache, vomiting, drowsiness, and stiffness in the neck and back progress to muscle weakness, spasms, and paralysis. Paralysis may be confined to one part of a limb or may be extensive and can include respiratory muscles.

There is no cure for polio, but prevention by vaccination (either Salk, which is injected, or Sabin, which is taken orally) is effective. New cases in the UK are uncommon today, but there are many people who contracted the disease before the vaccine became available, notably in the 1940s and 1950s.

Family living Most people with polio are disadvantaged to some extent by their disability. Access to buildings and the need for adaptations to the home may be major problems.

The need to keep warm may provide an additional financial burden to those who are already experiencing reduced income due to restricted opportunities in employment etc.

Psychological adjustment to disability demands special personal resources. Difficulty in obtaining information and support with post-polio problems may be worsened if socio-emotional problems remain.

Employment As severity of handicap varies greatly, people with polio may be found in the whole range of professions and occupations, but some may need sheltered workshop opportunities.

At one time many people with polio received education in special schools. Today, most attend mainstream schools. Polio does not affect intelligence level. Some people whose special schooling resulted in their not being able to obtain academic qualifications find their employment opportunities reduced.

Aids and benefits Aids centres run by the Disabled Living Foundation and occupational therapists from the social services departments can advise and offer information concerning a whole range of aids and adaptations. The progress made in electronic technology has made very specialised equipment available, and much greater independence is achieved by users of electronic aids.

Assistance towards the cost of electric wheelchairs, household equipment, heating expenses, stairlifts, hoists, driving lessons, holidays, etc. is often needed in addition to the help provided by the statutory departments.

Support agencies The British Polio Fellowship provides social activities through its local branches, a welfare service, holiday accommodation, a quarterly bulletin, and information leaflets.

Useful literature

- *Inside the iron lung*, Mimi Rudulph (Kensal Press, 1984)

Communication disorders

Autism

Introduction An American child psychiatrist, Leo Kanner, first described early-childhood autism in 1943.

The typical Kanner syndrome occurs in approximately 4 or 5 per 10 000 children, which means about 3000 children of school age with autism in the UK, but similar autistic features are also observed in a much larger number of children with different disabilities.

The condition usually begins from birth and rarely occurs later than three years old. The primary cause is still unknown.

Children with autism behave in strange and puzzling ways, have difficulties in relating to other people, and fail to make sense of the social world.

Main characteristics A child with autism seems to lack an awareness of other people as being a most important, significant, or interesting part of his or her surroundings. The young child pays more attention to objects than to people, but may be more responsive when older.

A major problem in understanding and using either verbal or non-verbal communication is also characteristic. Some children do not develop any useful language, or only use certain words or phrases in a rigid sense. There seems to be only a very literal and concrete interest in their environment.

A lack of imagination, flexible thought, or ideas means that most children with autism do not engage in imaginative play, and those that do tend to repeat activities over and over regardless of suggestions by other children or adults.

For some children with autism there may be an oversensitivity to certain sounds; fascination with bright lights, water, and spinning objects; and an indifference to pain, heat, or cold.

Abnormal body movements often associated with autism — such as grimacing, arm flapping, jumping, hopping from one foot to another, rocking, and charging in different directions at great speed — are usually made worse by excitability.

In relation to mental handicap, moderate learning difficulties occur in about one-quarter and severe learning difficulties in about one-half of all people with autism. The remainder have average or above average intelligence levels.

Causes   At first, theories tended to suggest that autism is related to an abnormality of emotional development. However, with a greater understanding of intellectual problems and their association with organic conditions, particularly in the more severely handicapped, the disorder is thought be one of cognition and language development.

It has been suggested that there is a defect in the ability to make coherent sense of the signals involved in communication. In particular, children with autism have difficulty in understanding gesture, facial expression, and tone of voice. In addition, about 50% of children with autism have handicaps from physical illness or injury affecting the brain and central nervous system.

Autism occurs in all parts of the world, but boys are affected more often than girls, in the ratio of 4 to 1.

Inheritance pattern   Most parents of children with autism have other children who are not autistic, and it is very rare for there to be more than one child with autism in a family. However, inheritance patterns are still a topic of research.

Diagnosis   Most children with autism look quite normal from birth, and parents become only slowly aware of difficulties during the first two years of life. Other people do not understand why the autistic child screams or behaves badly in public. Sleepless nights may be a regular occurrence in the early years. Feeding problems are fairly common, beginning with poor sucking after birth and sometimes leading to difficulties in chewing lumpy food etc.

In view of the very variable presentation of this condition, diagnosis can be difficult to ascertain as the underlying autistic problems may not always be obvious. For example, many children with autism are initially thought to have a hearing handicap or to be mentally handicapped. Diagnosis depends upon careful observation of the child and detailed history-taking, especially concerning early development. Parents often feel frustrated if the diagnosis is unclear and are relieved when the 'autistic' label can be given.

The basic impairments can occur in different degrees of severity and may change with age, and there may be associated handicaps such as physical disability, peripheral sensory impairments, epilepsy, mental handicap, etc. — all of which makes diagnosis that much more difficult.

Treatment   It may be necessary to use tranquillisers or other drugs in the short or long term.

Diet   It has been suggested that hyperactivity is associated with certain food dyes or additives. However, there is no real evidence to support this, although some families have found that their children react to certain foods. Changes in the body's immunity system may be triggered off by certain foods.

Family living   Many children with autism show attachment on a simple physical level to adults that they know well but may be indifferent to most adults and children of their own age.

Children with autism can appear socially immature, resist change, and exhibit very difficult behaviour in public. Living with a child with autism is made very wearing by temper tantrums, fits of screaming, making naive or embarrassing remarks, fear of harmless things together with a lack of fear of real danger, and the inability to understand social norms and rules. A worsening of difficult behaviour may occur in adolescence until early adult life.

The child with autism needs constant care, and this requires considerable patience and skill on the part of all family members. This can be very rewarding for both the child and his or her family, as much progress can be made with intensive care and education. For those children who learn to speak and to understand some language, the social withdrawal may become less acute with age, although the handicap prevents development to forming a mature relationship with another person.

The need for respite care and also more long-term provision is important for young people to gain some independence. A range of facilities is required to meet the needs of different ability groups.

The very special relationship which parents have with their child can be usefully developed by allowing and encouraging parental involvement or support in all outside activities. Families tend to feel that many professionals do not always fully understand the day-to-day reality of bringing up a child with autism, as this kind of understanding is not provided by textbook descriptions during training.

Education   Skills which do not involve language or abstract meaning can be developed, and most children with autism love music and singing and tend to be good at jigsaw puzzles and constructional toys which depend on an awareness of shape. Some children have the ability to remember words, dates, lists, etc. Regular routine is important, and tasks should not be too complex.

Pre-school activities are important, and attendance at a nursery or playgroup can help both the child and parents in finding ways of integrating into the community.

Special schools provided by the National Autistic Society have developed methods of teaching autistic children and managing difficult behaviour. Since 1971, several mainstream schools have taken a child with autism, but most autistic children attend schools for children with severe learning difficulties. The Invalid Children's Aid Association provides schools for children with communication disorders.

Most children with autism need specialised care and will eventually require residential care. It is important, however, that they receive the right kind of stimulation, in order to prevent disturbed, self-destructive, or aggressive behaviour.

School facilities for children with special needs are usually available at a local level, although the pattern of provision is very variable in different parts of the country. More specialised school and post-school facilities may be long distances away from home, which is a disadvantage for some autistic children and their families, although other children gain from the consistency and security that a residential facility can provide. Some parents feel that a change of environment and separation can be painful experiences for a child with autism.

It is most important that the education and social training in school is followed up after the child leaves, as the benefit in relation to social capabilities may be lost without continued reinforcement.

In general, people with autism require a much greater number of years in school, with an emphasis on social and educational training. Although much has been learnt about how to organise their environment to help develop potential skills and reduce behaviour problems, most people with autism are not able to become independent adults.

Further education and training   Local adult training centres are not always appropriate. There is a great need for provision of courses designed for students with special needs in colleges and centres, particularly where staff have very specialised knowledge and can cater for people with autism as well as students with different kinds of learning difficulties.

Employment   Some autistic children remain mute and withdrawn all their lives. The majority improve as they grow older and the world gradually becomes more understandable. Most adults continue to need care and supervision, but some find work in open or sheltered employment.

Aids and benefits   Parents and families need monetary support to compensate for the additional demands of care and to provide alternative carers when necessary. This is at present met in part by the attendance allowance, which many families find they can claim.

Support agencies The National Autistic Society (formed by parents in 1962 as the National Society for Autistic Children) aims to provide more day and residential centres concerned with education and training, to encourage research, and to stimulate greater understanding among professionals and the general public. It offers an advisory and information service for both parents and professionals. Seminars and conferences have become a regular feature of the work of the NAS.

A quarterly journal, *Communication*, is available from the NAS, together with useful publications. Local societies also provide a support and advisory network.

The National Autistic Society owns and manages several schools, some of which offer day, weekly, or termly facilities; hostels linked to a workshop; day centres; adolescent units attached to schools; family centres; etc.

Other relevant organisations include the Royal Society for Mentally Handicapped Children and Adults (Mencap) and the Invalid Children's Aid Association.

Useful literature
- *Children apart*, Lorna Wing (NAS, 4th edition 1984)
- *The handicaps of autistic children*, Lorna Wing (NAS)
- *Autistic children: a guide for parents*, Lorna Wing (Constable, 1980)
- *Involuntary strangers: a guide on autistic children for parents and professionals*, Peggie Everard (John Clare Books, 1980)

Dyslexia

Introduction The term 'dyslexia' is used to cover a wide range of handicaps, from mild spelling difficulties to complete illiteracy. Many people now prefer to refer to 'a specific learning difficulty'.

Dyslexia (or 'word blindness') can be distinguished from congenital auditory imperception ('word deafness'), the latter being a lack of speech resulting from an inability to comprehend the spoken word. Word deafness is often characterised by a failure of perception of the significance or meaning of sounds in the early years. Children frequently develop a vocabulary of their own. The condition is rare, and diagnosis is aided by modern audiological techniques which show a response to sound.

It is estimated that about 10% of children in the Western population have some form of dyslexia, and it seems to be more common among boys than girls.

Difficulties in reading and writing are common, and some children have difficulty with spatial orientation. Most also have trouble learning to spell correctly and to express thoughts on paper.

Main characteristics   There are degrees of this handicap. Some can read fluently, with symptoms only appearing in spelling form. Others read much more slowly and find difficulty when copying notes and answering examination questions. Reversals in letter orientation and sequence — e.g. 'dag' for 'bag' and 'form' for 'from' — are common.

Many children with early language and speech difficulties have subsequent reading, writing, spelling, and arithmetic problems.

Causes   Dyslexia is unrelated to intellect or social class, but the problem may seem more obvious in intelligent children.

Generally dyslexia is associated with a lack of established cerebral dominance. Normally one cerebral hemisphere is dominant such that the eye and hand on one side — usually the right — dominate the other. Where cross-laterality is present, the dominant eye is on the opposite side to the dominant hand.

Though not fully understood, it is thought that cross-laterality and the difficulties with reading and writing result from a disturbance in the very early development of cerebral function. Birth traumas such as temporary oxygen deprivation may be additional factors.

Inheritance pattern   There is some evidence to suggest that dyslexia is largely inherited. With improved assessment and awareness concerning dyslexia, it has been noticed that many children of mothers with dyslexia have since been diagnosed as having mild forms of dyslexia.

Diagnosis   When assessments by school psychologists confirm dyslexia, it is often a relief for the child that his or her condition is explained. Previously the frustrations of the condition may have provoked behaviour problems.

Due to lack of knowledge, many adults with dyslexia unfortunately received no special help while at school. Today, the need for early detection is recognised. Visual disorders need to be excluded. The school psychological service can help to make the initial diagnosis.

Although dyslexia remains a true disorder of visual perception and cognitive function, causing grave learning difficulties in childhood, there is a danger of classifying a child who appears to be a slow confused learner as having dyslexia. This appears to happen in spite of qualified help and assessment being available to children.

It is important that the child's dyslexic problems are recognised as early as possible, so that appropriate action may be taken to meet individual needs.

Treatment   Without early assistance, many children are limited by their disability. Remedial lessons from a specially trained teacher are necessary in conjunction with the usual lessons in mainstream schools.

One example of treatment is the American multisensory approach to reading, where the aim is to introduce sound and symbol relationships simultaneously with reading and writing. Children are also encouraged to listen to correct pronunciation, as malapropisms are common in the speech of those with dyslexia. Although there is no cure as such for dyslexia, specialist methods of teaching may greatly improve the condition. Some hospitals have dyslexia or learning-difficulties clinics.

Family living   It is important to try to increase confidence, as many children with dyslexia believe that they are stupid. Having often been labelled 'failures' in school, it is important to emphasise their good points.

Both parents and teachers need to realise that the child is not being awkward. There may be psychosomatic illnesses or a tendency to take time off from school or other activities due to the frustration of having to deal with a reading/writing problem in everyday life.

Education   Early identification of the problem greatly helps the parent, teacher, and child to work positively towards overcoming the dyslexia. The need for special educational provision was highlighted in the Warnock Report and subsequently the Education Act 1981, which requires local education authorities to provide appropriate services for children with specific learning disabilities.

In the education of children with dyslexia, special problems and difficulties need to be taken into consideration. For example, the Look — Say method of learning to read depends on word recognition and is thus difficult for children with dyslexia. The phonic methods are usually easier. Also, as children with dyslexia find it difficult to remember letter sequences, using a dictionary can be a major problem. Children who are dyslexic often find it difficult to make accurate calculations and to recall numbers in sequence.

Other problems within the school or home will clearly aggravate dyslexic problems for a child. Children who have frequent changes of school, or who for a variety of reasons suffer emotionally during their early childhood and have an additional specific learning difficulty, may become so disturbed that they are unable to benefit from crucial early learning.

Most LEAs have a wide range of services, to support individualised structured teaching appropriate to a child's needs. Ideally, peripatetic teachers should visit all pupils with dyslexia in mainstream schools. Some school examination boards now make special allowances for pupils with dyslexia, such as extra time to finish examinations.

Further education/Employment Continued assistance may be necessary even after leaving school. Many teenagers with dyslexia find that — although they can read, write, and spell adequately — they still have difficulty in gathering sense from their textbooks and do not express their ideas in writing as well as their peers.

Sometimes youngsters leave school without having been identified as dyslexic. Where, in addition, a lack of understanding, encouragement, and remediation has been experienced previously, adults may feel particularly frustrated, withdrawn, and depressed.

Assessment is possible through the specialist careers officer and the educational psychologist. For adults, there is a Manpower Services Commission area psychological service.

Local colleges often provide specialised courses through adult literacy programmes, which may include courses designed to assist those diagnosed as having dyslexia. The Dyslexia Institute provides special study-skills courses, as do the Hornsby Centre and the Helen Arkell Dyslexia Centre.

Some adults find that they are unable to meet the reading, spelling, and/or writing demands of their job or of everyday life. Specialist help — particularly using multisensory learning techniques — can assist. Learning spelling rules and word order may lessen syntax problems.

Typing is sometimes found easier than writing, and many people find that they prefer to dictate on to tape. Word processors are also found to be beneficial.

Support agencies The British Dyslexia Association (BDA) is the national body uniting local associations and other groups such as the Helen Arkell Dyslexia Centre (HADC) and The Hornsby Centre. The BDA offers a comprehensive counselling, information, and referral service for people with dyslexia, parents, and teachers.

The Dyslexia Institute offers an assessment and teaching service for children and adults at a number of centres throughout England. At several centres, adult evening classes and study-skills classes are run by the Institute.

The Invalid Children's Aid Association (ICAA) provides literature and specialist residential schools.

Both the BDA and the Royal Society of Arts run diploma courses for teachers on specific learning disability.

Useful literature

- *Overcoming dyslexia: a straightforward guide for families and teachers*, Beve Hornsby (Martin Dunitz, 1984)
- *People with dyslexia: report of the working party commission* (British Council for Rehabilitation of the Disabled, 1974)
- *Educational implications of disability — a guide for teachers*, Judith Male and Claudia Thompson (RADAR, 1985)
- *Teaching the non-reading dyslexic child*, Gill Cotterill (Learning Development Aids, 1985)
- *A practical guide to dyslexia*, Jean Blight (Egon Publishers, 1985)

The Helen Arkell Dyslexia Centre offers a series of books (1976) which includes the following titles:

- *The problems of sequencing and orientation*
- *The problem of reading*
- *The problem of handwriting*
- *The problem of spelling*
- *Dyslexia motivation*
- *Speech therapy and the dyslexic*

Metabolic disorders

Coeliac disease

Introduction The coeliac condition results from a sensitivity of the intestinal lining to gluten, which is a protein found in wheat, rye, barley, and possibly oats. Damage to the lining of the small intestine reduces the ability of the gut to absorb nutrients from food. This results in wasting, which may lead to severe illness resembling malnutrition.

Coeliac symptoms can occur at any age, but most are diagnosed between the ages of 30 and 45 years. It is suggested that on average the condition occurs in 1 in 1500 people in the UK.

Main characteristics A baby with a coeliac condition, after being weaned on to food containing gluten, may develop bulky, pale, foul-smelling stools and be likely to vomit after eating. There may be irritability and lethargy with a general failure to thrive.

Some children might not show the symptoms until they are older, or the condition might lie dormant until adulthood. Symptoms can vary greatly from one person to another, whether child or adult. Adults may not have any obvious gastro-intestinal symptoms but will invariably have abnormal results from a blood tests.

Inheritance pattern Genetic factors are important, and there is thought to be a 1 in 10 chance of finding coeliac disease in more than one member of the same family.

Women appear to be more commonly affected than men.

Diagnosis/Treatment Diagnosis is usually made by the gastroenterology department of a general hospital after a jejunal biopsy (examination of tissue from the small intestine) is performed.

Treatment involves strict adherence to a gluten-free diet, and initially vitamin or mineral supplements may also be necessary. A strict diet completely controls the coeliac condition and allows the intestine to return to normal. On this diet, which needs to be lifelong, a person can eventually recover full health and strength.

In approximately 16% of people with coeliac disease, other associated disorders may be found — notably auto-immune disorders such as diabetes type 1, certain thyroid disorders, rheumatoid arthritis, and ulcerative colitis.

Diet   A person with coeliac condition must not eat any type of food which contains flour or wheat, rye, barley, and possibly oats in any form. Care must be taken, as flour is often an ingredient in many tinned and packaged foods.

Special gluten-free flour, bread, biscuits, and pasta are available on a doctor's prescription, and naturally gluten-free foods can be purchased in ordinary shops.

Support agencies   The Coeliac Society helps those with coeliac disease. Local groups are found in many parts of the country.

Useful literature

● *The coeliac handbook* (The Coeliac Society)

Cystic fibrosis

Introduction   Cystic fibrosis (CF) is a hereditary and life-threatening disorder which chiefly affects the lungs and the digestive system in children and young adults. An estimated 1 in 2000 children born in the UK have CF. Before the advent of antibiotics, children usually died from pneumonia in the first year of life.

The condition produces a thickening of the mucus throughout the body. The lungs tend to become infected, and respiratory infections are a common complication. The sticky mucus tends also to clog the tiny ducts from the pancreas, affecting the flow of enzymes into the digestive tract. This leads to poor absorption of foods, so that it is difficult to put on weight and maintain normal growth rate.

The prospect of surviving into a reasonably healthy adult is improving, but this is dependent on early diagnosis and careful management throughout childhood.

Main characteristics   Shortly after birth the symptoms may be only slight, with perhaps a cough. The stools are extremely foul-smelling, which is characteristic of the presence of partially digested fat. The baby often fails to gain weight but develops a voracious appetite.

Repeated respiratory infections continue throughout life and are a major factor. Wheezing and breathing difficulties may be experienced, and some children develop chronic bronchitis. Sinusitis is fairly common.

Causes   CF is the most common inherited disease in North-Western Europe. Despite greater medical understanding, the precise biochemical fault which causes it is has not yet been identified.

Inheritance pattern   CF is known to be due to a single recessive gene and is the commonest genetically determined disorder affecting children in the UK. One child in about 1600 receives one of the abnormal genes from each parent. Such a child therefore has a double degree of the gene and will have the disorder from birth.

About 1 in 20 in the general population carry one of these abnormal genes. They will not have CF, but will be a carrier of the gene. When both parents are carriers, there is a 1 in 4 chance of their child having CF. There is also a 1 in 4 chance that the child will neither have CF nor be a carrier. In addition, there will be a 2 in 4 chance that the child will have one CF gene and thus be a carrier like his or her parents. Thus children who actually have CF have inherited the disorder from both parents, but the parents themselves are unaffected.

Diagnosis   Approximately 400 new cases of CF are diagnosed each year in the UK. However the average GP may see only one new case in his or her working life, and a physician may see one new case a year.

Diagnosis can now be undertaken more precisely through a sweat test. There is an increased concentration of sodium and chloride in the sweat of those with CF.

Two major problems from birth are a very high susceptibility to bacterial infection of the lungs and a malfunctioning of the pancreas which interferes with digestion and thus with growth. If not diagnosed and treated early, irreversible damage is caused to the child's lungs which will be fatal in most cases. Treatment after diagnosis must be continuous.

As a result of early diagnosis and effective treatment, an increasing number of children with CF are reaching young adulthood.

Frequently there is a family history of CF, but parents who are carriers cannot be detected until they have produced a child with CF. Pre-natal diagnosis is available at 18 weeks before birth, but, due to recent location

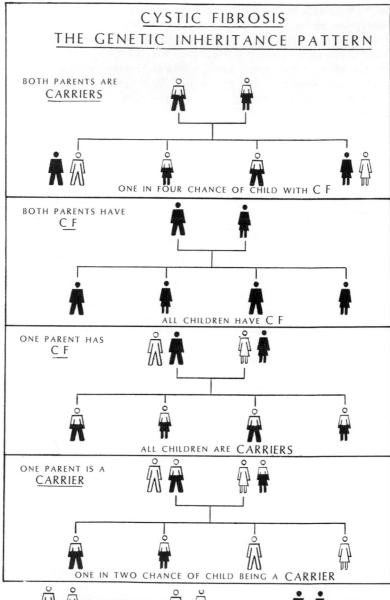

of the CF gene, an affected foetus can be detected at about the ninth week of pregnancy.

Following diagnosis, the family may be disbelieving and go through a period of denial, resentment, and guilt with regard to the hereditary factor. However, at all stages families find an opportunity for expression and discussion helpful.

Treatment In most cases, responsibility for management of CF is undertaken by the hospital with the consent of the GP. There are three main lines of treatment: dietary management, respiratory education and physiotherapy, and preventive control or treatment of bacterial infection.

Pancreatic enzyme replacements and other food supplements are taken with every meal throughout life, usually in the form of capsules or pills. The dosage is carefully worked out for each child.

Early diagnosis and prolonged antibiotic treatment of bacterial respiratory infection are essential. Long-term preventive antibiotic treatments may be recommended, as well as inhalation treatments.

Respiratory education and physiotherapy help expel mucus from the respiratory passages and lungs. Home physiotherapy taught to parents is vital in assisting drainage of lung secretions. In the first year of life, the child and parents should learn these techniques and use them at least twice daily, even if symptoms are not present. This then becomes part of the family routine.

Treatment is time-consuming, and children often find it tedious. Babies can be held over their parent's knee, but older children are best tipped over a wedge-shaped piece of foam or something similar (see the diagram below). Each session of physiotherapy gives obvious and immediate relief.

In the early years, parents may need to help with treatment, but as the child grows older, he or she can gradually become more independent. It is difficult to carry out home physiotherapy effectively throughout life, but limiting the extent of damage to lungs depends largely on keeping the respiratory tract clear through day-by-day treatment. However, most adolescents and adults are able to carry out their treatment independently and efficiently, having perfected the forced expiration techniques (self-percussion and breathing exercises).

Physical care and treatment are among the most important aspects of the management of CF. Physiotherapy is important in treating acute infection and preventing long-term injury to health.

Complications such as haemoptysis (coughing up blood) or pneumothorax (collapsed lung) may result and require hospital treatment.

Despite improved treatment techniques, CF can still prove fatal in early life, but, with improved treatment techniques, 75% reach late childhood or adolescence.

Positions for draining the lower parts of the lungs

Positions for draining lateral parts of the lungs

Position for draining the upper parts of the lungs

Fig. 5 Positions for physiotherapy in cystic fibrosis. (Physiotherapy is the single most important form of treatment in CF.)

Diet and exercise   In most cases of CF, no digestive juices enter the duodenum from the pancreas and 90% of all children with CF have an inability to digest and absorb normally. Pancreatin — in power, capsule, or pill form — has to be taken with every meal throughout life in a dosage carefully worked out for each person. Food absorption may still not be perfect, so a high-protein diet and an adequate supply of vitamins are then necessary. Moderate reduction in fat intake is also advisable, to avoid discomfort. In general, however, it is possible to maintain normal diet and growth, but, where necessary, special arrangements can usually be made in schools without difficulty.

Not every child with CF may be able to participate fully in physical activities. However, exercise does help to mobilise secretions.

Family living   For some people who have few symptoms and look fit and well, CF does not influence their lives greatly. Others will have suffered illness throughout childhood and have attended special schools and/or had an interrupted education. Most will have suffered taunting and unkind comments, and will have had to learn ways of coping with being 'different'.

Some children are very undersized and young-looking for their age. A very few have not reached puberty by their early twenties. Where puberty is reached at a normal age, the growth spurt is often delayed.

Adolescence is a particularly difficult time. Some supervision is still necessary, and parents may be overprotective of their children. Frustration at having to be dependent on parents for physiotherapy and care sometimes results in a rejection of treatment and denial of the condition.

The young person with CF is under the care of the hospital for the whole of his or her life, and families need support and encouragement from the professionals involved. For the majority there may be more than one child in the family affected, and very often a sibling has already died from the condition. The grief experienced by parents only adds to their anxieties and fears for the future. Parents often feel guilty that their child has distressing symptoms, frequent hospitalisation, and a restricted life. It is important that the child feels valued by his parents in spite of all these difficulties.

If taking part in the wider community means an increased risk of infection, these risks have to be balanced against the great advantages of leading a life similar to that of the child's contemporaries.

It is vital that children with CF are not subjected to damp or other health dangers. There may thus be a need for rehousing etc.

Education Children with CF have a normal range of intellectual ability and no difficulties with mobility or communication skills. They can thus integrate into a mainstream school, provided that the teaching staff are aware of their special needs. It is useful for parents to make an appointment with the school to discuss diet, medication, participation in PE, etc.

Home tuition or attendance at a special school has to be considered for only a small percentage of children — usually because there have been frequent absences because of illness, or as a temporary measure. If children need regular physiotherapy in addition to that provided by parents at home, special-school education may be more adequately able to provide the right facilities and a more relaxed environment. However, this may mean travelling further and/or attending a residential school. The sheltered and perhaps overprotected school years may make it more difficult for a child to adjust to group activities. A working co-operation between school, hospital, parents, etc. gives families the support and guidance they need.

Consideration of possible careers needs to begin at a much earlier age than usual.

Further education and training   If adequately informed, colleges will accommodate and make special arrangements for students with health problems.

For a minority of those with CF, attendance at a special rehabilitation centre for assessment and moving on to a special training centre may be appropriate.

Employment   It is important that the young person is accepted into a full working role rather than being classified as 'disabled'. Wherever possible, a young person with CF should be enrolled as a permanent member of staff with the usual pensions, insurance, and other benefits.

It is advisable to avoid lengthy commuting in crowded public transport or working in a damp and dusty atmosphere. Part-time or home-based occupations may, for a few people, be preferable.

Aids and benefits   People with CF are eligible for the attendance allowance.

Support agencies   The Cystic Fibrosis Research Trust has a network of over 200 branches and support groups throughout the UK. It provides a useful range of literature for parents and professionals.

Brompton hospital in London is the largest clinic in Europe providing direct access to a specialist team for young people suffering from CF.

Useful literature

● *Cystic fibrosis: manual of diagnosis and management*, John Dodge and Mary Goodchild (Baillière Tindall, 1985)

Diabetes

Introduction   Known since biblical times as the 'wasting disease', diabetes is one of the oldest known disabilities.

Diabetes occurs in both children and adults and can begin at any age. There are estimated to be over a million people with diabetes in the UK (i.e. 2% of the population) and about 30 000 new cases are diagnosed each year. More than 1500 children develop diabetes each year, and there are approximately 30 000 with diabetes under the age of 16 years. It is thought that many cases are undiagnosed — probably in the region of 600 000.

The handicap is unseen, but there is a vital daily dependence on insulin or specialised dietary control.

Although there is no known cure, treatment and understanding have greatly improved, notably since the 1920s. Diabetes is now medically controllable, but it can be serious if not properly treated.

Main characteristics Early symptoms include excessive thirst, frequent passing of urine, and loss of weight in children — but quite often there is an increase in weight in adults where there is a late onset.

Secondary complications which may arise are visual impairment, heart trouble, kidney damage, and gangrene. (One in 5 of the people under 65 registered blind each year have a visual impairment due to diabetes.)

A child whose insulin level is allowed to drop dramatically would eventually fall into a *hyper*glycaemic coma and die. (Before 1921, when insulin injections became available, most people with diabetes died in a coma.)

Excessive amounts of insulin can also cause problems. *Hypo*glycaemia is a condition of too little sugar in the blood, which may occur if there is an overactive production of insulin or as a result of an overdose of insulin (insulin hypoglycaemia). It can also occur when someone fails to eat after insulin treatment. Those people who have hypoglycaemia (when the blood-sugar level falls) may experience dizziness, confusion, blurred vision, etc. and it is important that they carry sugar or glucose with them.

If a person with diabetes is in a coma, that coma may be due to hyperglycaemia or hypoglycaemia. A useful clue is that the skin is usually sweaty in hypoglycaemia and dry in hyperglycaemia. To avoid hypoglycaemia coma setting in, sugar lumps or a sugar drink must be taken. However, it is vital not to feed or try to feed an unconscious person. In a situation where the person is in a coma and no doctor is available, rectal administration of glucose may be life-saving.

It is important for people with diabetes to carry a special diabetic card, to ensure prompt and correct treatment in an emergency.

Causes In most cases, the basic cause of diabetes is the failure of the pancreas gland to produce insulin, but the reason for this is not fully understood. This results in an abnormally high level of sugar being produced in the blood (hyperglycaemia), as it is the insulin's job to control the amount of sugar in the body.

Although partly due to a genetic defect, it is thought that in children viruses may also play a part.

Type-1 diabetes requires insulin injections, and this condition usually starts before 30 years of age. Type-2 diabetes is the more common adult-onset kind which requires control by diet and medication.

Inheritance pattern   Genetic factors may sometimes be relevant especially in younger people. However it is only the predisposition to diabetes which is inherited.

For those with type-1 diabetes, the overall risk of brothers and sisters developing diabetes is about 1 in 13. If one parent has type-1 diabetes, the risk to the child is 1 in 50. If both parents have diabetes, the risk is about 1 in 8.

Diagnosis   Childhood diabetes accounts for about 5% of all people with diabetes. Onset is usually from about two years of age. A great need for fluid and irritability because of dehydration together with enuresis (involuntary passing of urine) may be presenting features. Abdominal pain and vomiting may also occur. As a diabetic coma develops, there is increasing drowsiness and dehydration. It is thus important that diagnosis is made as early as possible, as this helps reduce complications of diabetes.

Families do not always properly understand their doctor's advice given at the traumatic moment of diagnosis. Several visits to the clinic are needed to establish the necessary support services and to help the family learn the treatment techniques of subcutaneous therapy (i.e. insulin injections). Management by diet alone may be insufficient, and oral preparations by themselves are unsuitable for children.

In view of the possible genetic factor, parents are usually encouraged to take other children in the family to the clinic for a blood test, especially when a child is ill with an infection.

Treatment   For children with diabetes, the close co-operation between parent and doctor is of paramount importance. Regular medical check-ups are very necessary — there are over 800 recognised diabetic clinics in the UK.

There are three main patterns of treatment:

i) Insulin injection plus diet and exercise is suitable for over 30% of cases — mostly young adults and children.

ii) A combination of tablets and diet is suitable mainly for the middle-aged and elderly. The tablets stimulate the production of insulin.

iii) Diet alone may be suitable for the middle-aged and elderly, especially if overweight.

A regular record of urine tests gives a good indication of the diabetic control, although blood-sugar testing is more precise. Regular weighing is also helpful in assessing control. Obesity (overweight) aggravates the long-term effects of diabetes. These tests can be done by the person at home, following instruction from the clinic.

Langwith Lodge at Mansfield is a convalescent home which offers specialised care for both men and women with diabetes.

Diet and exercise In recent years there has been an important emphasis on diet in the treatment of diabetes. A high-fibre is now thought to be particularly helpful. Eating out in restaurants becomes less of problem once basic food values are learnt. It is crucial to cut down on drinking alcohol and smoking tobacco. Exercise is very important. Once the diabetes has been controlled, most people can participate in all forms of sport. In fact to keep healthy requires regular insulin, regular exercise, regular meals, and regular medical supervision.

Family living For many families, public ignorance can be a major problem affecting employment, education, insurance, travel, etc.

All children who develop diabetes depend for their lives on daily insulin injections. However, the adjustment to a lifelong need for daily injections is not always easy for children to accept. Children, in particular, may find having to keep to a well-calculated diet a social embarrassment and limitation

Where the diabetes is unstable, the stress on the family can be particularly pronounced. In certain situations, residential schooling may be appropriate.

For elderly people who live alone, especially those who have added complications such as failing sight, diabetes can be particularly distressing.

There is a local need for greater short-term accommodation for rehabilitative and recuperative holidays.

Once the person has adjusted to the need for regular treatment and dietary requirements, a full and active life becomes possible.

Mobility It is important for those people using insulin injections to understand the relevant statutory requirements before driving a vehicle.

Education A large majority of children with diabetes attend mainstream schools. However it is important that the individual diabetic diet is understood by the school staff. A 'School Pack' is available from the British Diabetic Association which includes general advice on precautions to be taken with young diabetics on a day-to-day basis.

Employment There are people with diabetes in every type of occupation. However, certain types of employment are not possible for those who need insulin injections — bus driving, working with dangerous machinery, or jobs where individual safety and that of others may be put at risk, for example. Once the diabetes has been properly stabilised, it is usual for the person to continue working up to retirement age.

Aids and benefits In some cases the attendance allowance is appropriate. For those on a low income, it may be possible to obtain a small additional amount towards the cost of a diabetic diet if in receipt of social-security benefit.

Support agencies   The British Diabetic Association (BDA) offers practical advice and information to families and professionals. This includes dietary and welfare advisory services, educational holidays for both the young and the elderly, and seminars for parents and families. There are over 300 branches and parent groups throughout the UK. A magazine, *Balance*, is published bimonthly.

The BDA has a medical and scientific section and a professional-services section, as well as a youth department, a diabetic care department, and an education section.

The Invalid Children's Aid Association (ICAA) can also provide assistance and advice.

Useful literature

- *The diabetics handbook* (BDA, 1983)
- *Diabetes explained*, Arnold Bloom (MTP Press, 1982)
- *Cooking the new diabetic way* (BDA, 1983)
- *Life with diabetes*, Arnold Bloom (Family Doctor Publications, 1972)
- *Well being: diabetes* (Channel Four Television, 1983)
- *Diabetes mellitus*, R.J. Jarrett (Croom Helm, 1986)

Phenylketonuria

Introduction   Phenylketonuria (PKU) is a metabolic disorder which prevents the normal use of protein food. If untreated, it usually damages the nervous systems and leads to mental retardation.

PKU was first described in 1934 by I.A. Folling, a Norwegian physician, who noticed that some mentally retarded children excreted phenylpyruvic acid (phenylketone) in their urine. It was later found that, due to an inherited defect in an enzyme called phenylalanine hydroxylase (found mainly in the liver), the body of a child with PKU cannot dispose of the amino acid phenylalanine, resulting from the body's breaking down of any proteins consumed, in the usual way. Instead, this substance accumulates in the body, leading to brain damage.

In 1953 a diet low in phenylaline was found to prevent intellectual deterioration while maintaining normal growth. The average incidence of PKU throughout the UK is around 1 in 10 000 births, but the incidence will vary from area to area.

Main characteristics Progressive mental deterioration sets in from a few weeks of age.
Vomiting, irritability, and convulsions may result from the accumulation of toxic metabolites. Skin irritation is common. The urine has a musty smell, from the phenylpyruvic acid.

Inheritance pattern A child will develop PKU only if *both* parents are carriers. It is not uncommon to be a carrier for PKU, as about 1 in 50 people possess one altered PKU gene. The likelihood of both parents being carriers is however only about 1 in 3000. In each pregnancy there is then a 1 in 4 chance that the baby will have PKU (and an equal chance that the child will be normal) but a 2 in 4 chance that the child will be a carrier like the parents. Thus there are a few parents who have more than one child with PKU and some who are not aware that they are carriers as none of their children has been affected.
There is a high risk that babies born to mothers with PKU may be mentally and physically handicapped at birth. Control of blood phenylalanine levels by a strict low-phenylalanine diet — started well before conception and continued throughout pregnancy — will greatly reduce this risk. It is thus particularly important that families understand the genetic implications and that young women with PKU seek counselling before planning a pregnancy.

Diagnosis A comprehensive screening process identifies PKU in the first weeks of life. This simple test is routinely carried out on all infants between the sixth and fourteenth day after birth.
If PKU is diagnosed, it may be necessary for the baby to remain in hospital until the phenylalanine level is low and the child is gaining weight satisfactorily.

Treatment Children maintained on the correct diet develop normally, both physically and intellectually. The hospital paediatrician and dietician help to prepare a low-phenylalanine diet.
Frequent blood tests (taken at home) and regular visits to the clinic are necessary to monitor progress and make appropriate adjustments in the diet. The child is particularly vulnerable up to the age of two years.
If the treatment is not started early or maintained carefully, then brain damage is most likely to occur.

Diet When a child with PKU follows a normal diet containing rela-

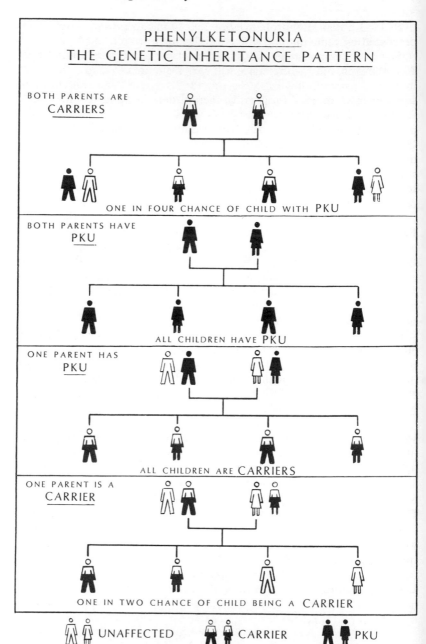

PHENYLKETONURIA
THE GENETIC INHERITANCE PATTERN

BOTH PARENTS ARE
CARRIERS

ONE IN FOUR CHANCE OF CHILD WITH PKU

BOTH PARENTS HAVE
PKU

ALL CHILDREN HAVE PKU

ONE PARENT HAS
PKU

ALL CHILDREN ARE CARRIERS

ONE PARENT IS A
CARRIER

ONE IN TWO CHANCE OF CHILD BEING A CARRIER

UNAFFECTED   CARRIER   PKU

tively large amounts of protein, phenylalanine accumulates. This can be prevented by reducing the amount of natural protein in the diet and replacing it with a protein food specially prepared for people with PKU. As well as this low-phenylalanine protein supplement, the diet must include low-protein/high-calorie supplements and vitamin and mineral supplements. Many of these are available on prescription.

This diet is started as soon as diagnosis is confirmed, and it is usually possible to maintain breast-feeding if this has been established. Opinions vary on relaxation of the diet, but it is generally considered that, after the initial years of strict control, there can be some relaxation some time after eight years of age, although some restriction may be beneficial throughout life. Management of the diet will depend on the particular needs and circumstances of the individual person.

Family living At birth, the initial trauma for parents of a child diagnosed as having PKU involves feelings of confusion, anxiety, and failure. Learning to come to terms with the rather restrictive diet and its associated problems takes time. The problems may at first seem insurmountable, and it is helpful if parents can have contact with another family who have a child with PKU, usually through the health visitor or the voluntary organisation concerned with PKU.

Later it is sometimes difficult to maintain a varying diet to suit each child's likes and dislikes, and the problem of explaining special diet arrangements to friends, school staff, etc. can cause the child to feel different and in a few instances to rebel against the dietary restrictions. Co-operation and understanding are important on the part of the whole family, friends, and the care team.

Benefits Families with a child who has PKU with additional learning difficulties may find that they meet the criteria for the attendance allowance.

Support agencies The National Society for Phenylketonuria and Allied Disorders (NSPKU) aims to provide social and educational support to families. Contact between families is arranged through the Society, which also has a regular newsletter and offers publications and information in general.

Useful literature

● *The child with phenylketonuria*, John Holton and Linda Tyfield (NSPKU, 1986)

Blood disorders

Haemophilia

Introduction The term 'haemophilia' is used in a wide sense to describe a group of inherited blood disorders in which there is a life-long defect in one of the clotting factors which cause blood to coagulate and hence stop bleeding. The commonest of these disorders — classical haemophilia — is transmitted by both sexes but (except in rare circumstances) causes bleeding only in the male.

The clotting factors present in blood are numbered from I to XIII. The clotting factor which is defective in haemophilia A is factor VIII. Haemophilia B or 'Christmas disease' affects factor IX. Von Willebrand's syndrome, which affects both sexes, is less common and is a combination of deficiency in clotting factor VIII together with an abnormal functioning of the platelets in the blood, which fail to form an adequate plug of a wound to stop bleeding.

The severity of the haemophilic condition is generally related to the degree of deficiency of the relevant clotting factor in the blood. Characteristically, von Willebrand's syndrome is less clinically severe.

Approximately 1 in 8000 people in the UK have some form of haemophilia.

Main characteristics Bleeding will occur for much longer than normal after injury or operations. Those severely affected with haemophilia A or B also bleed spontaneously into joints and elsewhere in the body. For each person, spontaneous bleeds can vary in frequency from three or more times a week to three times a year. An increase in the frequency of bleeds may be directly related to a period of emotional trauma.

An ache, irritation, or tingling in an affected area leads to definite pain, stiffness, and limitation of use, and the site of the bleed will become hot, swollen, and progressively more tender. Prompt treatment can reduce progressive damage to joints which would otherwise result in severe arthritis and deformity. These are present to a greater extent in older people who have not benefited from modern treatment methods. In mild haemophilia, bruising may only occur following knocks and bangs.

Inheritance pattern The genetic inheritance pattern of haemophilia has special implications within the family, yet, although there is often a history of the disorder in the family, many may be unaware of it. Haemophilia can also occur as a mutation.

When a man with haemophilia has children, none of his sons will have haemophilia nor can they pass on the condition. However, all his daughters will be carriers. A carrier is someone who can hand on the condition without suffering from it. With each pregnancy, the daughter carrier will have a 1 in 2 chance of a son having haemophilia and likewise a 1 in 2 chance of a daughter being a carrier.

Carrier detection tests are available but are not totally reliable at present.

Diagnosis Diagnosis of severe haemophilia is usually made in childhood. The first sign may be that a child beginning to walk or crawl is found to bruise very easily. Prolonged bleeding after injury, even continuing for several days, may also occur.

If there is a family history, parents may be aware of the possibility that their child might be affected and tests can be arranged and diagnosis be made at a very early stage. It is now possible to take a blood sample from a male foetus at 18 to 20 weeks and directly determine whether haemophilia is present. This has provided much better information for women unsure about continuing their pregnancy.

Some parents have no family history or perhaps were not aware of the possibility of haemophilia. In such instances, many will have suffered a period of anxiety, conflict, and frustration before their child's condition is diagnosed as haemophilia. Parents are often relieved to find that haemophilia-centre staff are familiar with their child's condition. It is impossible to impart all the necessary information in one initial interview, and several meetings at the haemophilia centre are needed.

Treatment Every person with haemophilia carries a special card and must attend a haemophilia centre for treatment and supervision. There are about ten major reference centres in the UK.

Effective treatment has only been readily available since 1965. Now, prompt treatment by an intravenous injection of a concentrated form of the appropriate clotting factor obtained from whole blood is vital to reduce progressive damage to joints. Open access on a 24-hour basis is available within centres, and the emergency ambulance service can be used. The effect of each dose lasts only a few hours but, given promptly,

HAEMOPHILIA
THE GENETIC INHERITANCE PATTERN

FATHER HAS
HAEMOPHILIA

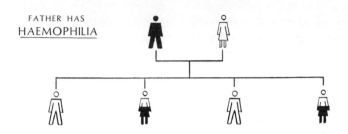

ALL DAUGHTERS ARE CARRIERS

MOTHER IS A
CARRIER

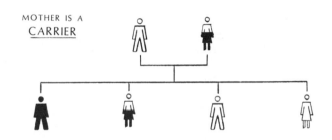

ONE IN TWO CHANCE OF SON HAVING HAEMOPHILIA
ONE IN TWO CHANCE OF DAUGHTER BEING A CARRIER

UNAFFECTED   CARRIER   HAEMOPHILIA

one infusion will usually stop the bleed. Once the bleeding stops, pain rapidly diminishes and use of the limb returns.

For some people, treatment supplies can be used at home, and this greatly improves a person's ability to participate in school, work, social activities, etc. with little interruption. Home treatment is an ideal method, as a minimum amount of time is lost between the recognition of a bleed and treatment. These treatment products can be stored in an ordinary refrigerator.

Supplies of concentrate are not sufficient to treat all actual bleeding episodes and can seldom be used to prevent bleeding. National Health Service supplies are, however, expected to reach self-sufficiency for minimum needs in the near future.

About 5 to 10% of all people with haemophilia develop inhibitors which prevent present treatment products being effective. Alternative treatment products may soon be available.

With prompt treatment now available to most, the level of pain experienced should not warrant strong painkillers. However, individuals' pain thresholds differ. While no person should suffer needlessly, dependence problems can arise if strong analgesics are prescribed for every bleeding episode.

While there is reason for people with haemophilia to be concerned about the risks of contracting hepatitis or AIDs through blood transfusions, the risks are low and research progress suggests that alternative non-blood products may be available in the future.

Family living   From the moment haemophilia is diagnosed, support and guidance for the family are important, particularly to families who are finding it difficult to adapt to their new situation. Mothers may experience a severe initial guilt reaction which encourages overprotection and a feeling of obligation to take on all the responsibilities for her son's care. How parents resolve their feelings will thus greatly influence their own and other family members' attitudes towards the haemophilic child.

A balance must be achieved between protection and allowing the child to grow up into a well adjusted and healthy adult. Parents who are not reassured may respond by imposing unnecessary restrictions.

General support from the health visitor, family doctor, social worker, and others is of paramount importance in addition to the link maintained between the family and the haemophilia-centre care team. The interruptions to day-to-day living and pressures caused by the need for immediate treatment put heavy demands on the family.

Mobility   Mobility for the older person who has not benefited from the improved treatment products is likely to be restricted by progressively arthritic joints. Crutches may be needed, particularly during a bleeding episode. Generally for younger people, where prompt treatment has been regularly received, reduced mobility is likely to occur for only a limited period shortly after a bleeding episode has begun. However, many people with haemophilia are eligible for the mobility allowance, and a safe means of transport can be a crucial factor if risks of injury are to be avoided.

Education　Most children with haemophilia attend and cope well in mainstream schools. Education is vitally important, as it is not advisable to rely on manual employment.

School heads should be fully informed of the nature of haemophilia and have an opportunity to discuss the haemophilic boy's difficulties with his parents. Haemophilia is comparatively rare, therefore the school doctor may not be familiar with the condition. The haemophilia centre will provide information and clarification to staff within the school.

One of the main problems is loss of school work due to visits to hospital or periods of rest at home following bleeds. These problems may be accentuated where the nearest haemophilia centre is many miles away. However, where home treatment is allowed, time lost from school is reduced, and many children lose attendance only in exceptional circumstances.

For a few children, education at a special school may seem more appropriate. These schools offer a more sheltered atmosphere, physiotherapy, individual care and supervision, and an understanding of special problems. Few special schools have treatment facilities for children with haemophilia on or near their premises, so time lost from school continues to be a problem. However, there are two residential schools which provide treatment facilities: Lord Mayor Treloar College (Hampshire) and Welburn Hall School (Yorkshire).

Leaving school can be a stressful period, as a boy will be entering a community which has comparatively little understanding of haemophilia.

Further education and training　Many people with haemophilia move into further education and undertake professional careers. This is made easier and less stressful if the person is receiving home therapy.

Employment　Most children with haemophilia attend and cope well in mainstream schools, and the choice of employment is made considerably easier if a reasonably high standard of education has been reached. Early careers advice is essential.

In each case, the choice of occupation is related to the severity of haemophilia. Generally appropriate occupations are those which are not physically demanding and in which there is a low risk of injury.

The vast majority of doubts and prejudices as far as the employer is concerned stem from ignorance concerning the nature of the disability. Superficial cuts need only a little extra pressure and a sticking plaster, while a severe injury will require hospital attention, just as it would for anyone else.

Many people find that the frequency of bleeds is lowered once they are settled in satisfying employment. Anxiety increases the frequency of bleeding episodes, and the possibility of finding regular work then becomes more difficult. This can lead to other problems unrelated to haemophilia if work is difficult to find or keep. Negative attitudes to work and life can prove to be as great a bar to employment as the physical disability itself.

Advances in medical treatment have resulted in dramatic changes to the lives of families with young haemophilic children. Home treatment has provided young people with the key to leading a more independent life and benefiting physically and emotionally from prompt and effective treatment. For this reason, few choose to register as disabled.

Aids and benefits Many families find that they are able to claim for whole or part of the attendance allowance. Also, the mobility allowance is frequently appropriate.

Support agencies The social worker within the social services department of the hospital is often the link person between the haemophilia centre, outside community agencies, and the family.

The Haemophilia Society provides general advice and information and details of specially arranged caravan holidays. Leaflets for families and for professionals involved in the care of haemophilia are also available. Local support groups throughout the UK are an important source of information, contact between families, etc.

There is a British Association of Social Workers (BASW)/Haemophilia Society special interest group for social workers which holds yearly conferences for all professionals involved. Further information may be obtained from the haemophilia centre at the Royal Free Hospital, London (01-794 0500).

Useful literature

- *Introduction to haemophilia* (The Haemophilia Society, 1984)
- *Living with haemophilia*, Peter Jones (MTP Press, 1984)
- *AIDS: questions and answers*, V.G. Daniels (Cambridge Medical Books, 1986)
- *Proceedings of the AIDS conference, January 1986*, ed. Peter Jones (Intercept, 1986)
- *AIDS: nursing guidelines* (Royal College of Nursing, 1985)
- *Touch me who dares*, Lionel F. Shelley (Gomer Press, 1985)

Leukaemia

Introduction   Leukaemia is a rare disease which affects the blood. Advances in treatment are being made all the time and in some cases leukaemia can be cured; in most, life can be prolonged.

Leukaemia is a cancer of the blood which is caused by an overproduction of abnormal or immature white blood cells. It may start in the bone marrow or the lymph system. Bone marrow is one of the places where blood cells are made and these may be red cells (which carry oxygen), white cells (which fight infection), or platelets (which form clots to prevent bleeding).

Immature white cells are known as myelocytes and, as myelocytes are mainly found in the bone marrow, leukaemia which starts in the bone marrow is called myeloid leukaemia.

Another type of white blood cell, called lymphocytes, are made mainly in the lymph nodes (although some are made in the bone marrow). Leukaemia of the lymph system is therefore known as lymphatic leukaemia.

There are several different forms of leukaemia — some more commonly affect the young rather than the elderly, and vice versa.

Leukaemia is relatively uncommon, occurring in approximately 10 per 1 000 000 population until the age of 75 and about 50 per 1 000 000 thereafter.

Main characteristics/Diagnosis   There are four types of leukaemia which are the most common: acute myeloid, acute lymphatic, chronic myeloid, and chronic lymphatic leukaemia.

Acute leukaemias occur in adults as well as children. However, the acute lymphatic leukaemia is more common in children. Incidence is 50 per 1 000 000 between the ages of 2 to 4 years, with a secondary peak in adults after 65 years.

Chronic myeloid leukaemia is found in adults and only occasionally in children. Chronic lymphatic leukaemia affects mainly older people (particularly males), and the average age of onset is 65 years.

Generally speaking, leukaemia is more common in males than in females.

The most common symptoms are anaemia, fatigue, low resistance to infection, bruising, and nose bleeds. For each person these symptoms vary in severity.

The symptoms progress very rapidly in acute leukaemia, whereas in chronic leukaemia the symptoms may appear only gradually and it is some time before diagnosis can be reached. In some cases the diagnosis of chronic leukaemia may be made by chance, for example when a person goes to hospital for another reason.

Following diagnosis, it is usual to give information concerning the implications of the leukaemia and its treatment to families.

Causes   The cause of leukaemia is unknown in the majority of cases, although radiation and some chemicals may be responsible in a small percentage. It is suggested that it may be the result of a virus.

Leukaemia is not contagious, nor is it inherited, but there is a higher incidence in identical twins and among children with Down's syndrome.

Treatment   Once an accurate diagnosis and classification of the cell-type have been made, the appropriate treatment can be given.

The aim of treatment in acute leukaemia is to clear the abnormal or immature cells from the blood and almost completely from the marrow. The phases of treatment are divided into remission induction, consolidation, and maintenance. Most people with leukaemia are treated with drugs (chemotherapy) throughout each of these phases. Once remission has been achieved, it may in a few cases be possible to suitably match donors for a bone-marrow transplant.

It is important that close supervision is given in order to monitor any infection that may develop.

Some people will experience relapse, when the leukaemia cells build up again in spite of the drugs, and this relapse remains a major problem in the management of the condition.

Prognosis is improving all the time, due to a better understanding of the condition and its management. Many children have survived for many years following diagnosis of acute lymphatic leukaemia. However the average duration of survival for those with acute myeloid leukaemia is only about two years.

Most young adults (below 45 years) can expect to achieve remission, but prognosis in adults is poor. The older the age, the less are the chances of remission occurring. Remissions can last anything from 2 months to a number of years.

Family living   Children and adults have a remarkable capacity for coming to terms with a condition such as leukaemia. The anxiety and sense of loss that families experience once diagnosis is made, together with the demands made by the treatment process, create a situation where a great deal of support is needed, particularly from hospital staff. Most treatment units are supported by a social worker who is an integral member of the care team.

There are a great many children who have survived many years after diagnosis of leukaemia. Most such children show normal growth and development and sexual maturation, and several girls have given birth to healthy babies.

It is important that families are allowed to have future expectations and to plan ahead in the hope that the child or adult will reach remission where a reasonable prognosis can be maintained.

Education   A great deal of time is lost in school due to long periods of hospitalisation. Most children with leukaemia attend mainstream schools, however.

Employment   The outlook for children and young adults with lymphatic leukaemia has improved such that many can realistically consider entering careers of their own choice. It seems that, in general, employers have not been reluctant to consider applicants who have been treated for leukaemia.

Support agencies   The Leukaemia Care Society was formed in 1967 by a small group of parents. The Society offers reassurance and support to families, information and literature, financial grants, etc. The Leukaemia Research Fund is based at the Hospital for Sick Children in London.

Useful literature

The Leukaemia Research Fund provides a wide range of literature, including.

● *A guide to the treatment and care of childhood leukaemia*
● *Leukaemia in adults*
● *Leukaemia in children*

Sickle cell disease

Introduction   Sickle cell disease is the name given to a group of inherited disorders of haemoglobin formation. These include sickle cell anaemia, haemoglobin SC disease, and sickle cell β-thalassaemia. The most common of these is sickle cell anaemia and this text therefore concentrates on this disorder, although most of the information also applies to other sickling disorders.

In the UK, sickle cell anaemia is common in people of African or West Indian (Caribbean) descent. One in 10 such people have sickle cell trait and 1 in 300 have sickle cell anaemia.

It may also occur in people from the Eastern Mediterranean, the Middle East, India, and Pakistan. It is suggested that the geographical distribution has probably arisen because sickle cell trait offers some protection against malaria. Sickle cell anaemia, however, does not.

Main characteristics Sickle cell anaemia makes people prone to bouts of anaemia, pain, jaundice, or infection. These are called 'crises'. Crises can occur quite often or maybe only once every few years. Pain can sometimes be severe and is usually in the arms, legs, back, and stomach. There may be some swelling of the hands and feet and painful or stiff joints. People with sickle cell anaemia are prone to coughs, colds, sore throats, and fever, or to more serious infections and illnesses such as pneumonia and septicaemia (blood poisoning). Sickling can also occur in the lungs and eyes.

At times the anaemia will get worse, causing lethargy and general malaise. Other problems include mild jaundice, enuresis, and delayed puberty.

Sickle cell anaemia does not usually affect intelligence, except in the rare event of a severe stroke.

Causes There are over 300 different types of haemoglobin, a protein which is contained in red blood cells. Haemoglobin A (HbA) is the most common type and is the one most people inherit from both their parents (HbAA). If however most of the haemoglobin inherited is sickle haemoglobin (HbS), the person will develop sickle cell anaemia. The name comes from the sickle or crescent shape the red blood cells take on when they give up oxygen. These cells are removed more quickly from circulation than normal red blood cells, leading to anaemia.

Haemoglobin SC disease and sickle cell β-thalassaemia occur when one parent passes on sickle haemoglobin and the other passes on either haemoglobin C or β-thalassaemia. The symptoms are similar to sickle cell anaemia, although usually less severe.

Inheritance pattern If a person inherits sickle haemoglobin from only one parent, he or she will have sickle cell trait (HbAS). Sickle cell trait is symptom-free and cannot turn into sickle cell disease. However, if both parents are carriers of sickle cell trait, there is a 1 in 4 chance that each of their children could be born with sickle cell anaemia. There is a 2 in 4 chance that the child may have sickle cell trait and a 1 in 4 chance that the child may not be affected at all.

Thus, if a person inherits sickle haemoglobin from both parents, he or she will have sickle cell anaemia (HbSS).

Diagnosis A specific blood test can identify sickle cell trait and sickle cell disease. A family history also aids clarification. Repeated attacks of jaundice may be an indication of sickle cell anaemia for those people in high-risk groups.

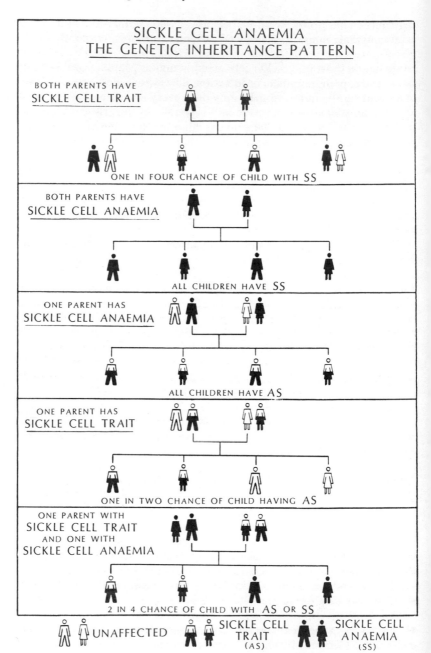

SICKLE CELL ANAEMIA
THE GENETIC INHERITANCE PATTERN

BOTH PARENTS HAVE
SICKLE CELL TRAIT

ONE IN FOUR CHANCE OF CHILD WITH SS

BOTH PARENTS HAVE
SICKLE CELL ANAEMIA

ALL CHILDREN HAVE SS

ONE PARENT HAS
SICKLE CELL ANAEMIA

ALL CHILDREN HAVE AS

ONE PARENT HAS
SICKLE CELL TRAIT

ONE IN TWO CHANCE OF CHILD HAVING AS

ONE PARENT WITH
SICKLE CELL TRAIT
AND ONE WITH
SICKLE CELL ANAEMIA

2 IN 4 CHANCE OF CHILD WITH AS OR SS

UNAFFECTED   SICKLE CELL
TRAIT
(AS)   SICKLE CELL
ANAEMIA
(SS)

Treatment It is possible to help reduce the frequency and severity of crises and their complications by prompt recognition and treatment. It is important to maintain good general health and diet. Infections should be treated in the initial stages, and children in particular should be kept warm and dry to reduce colds etc. They may be given a regular small dose of antibiotics. In addition, they will need analgesics (painkillers) to deal with the painful crisis. People with sickle cell anaemia experience dehydration and must take plenty of fluids. Supplements of folic acid (a B vitamin) can be helpful. Regular haemoglobin tests and hospital follow-up appointments are essential.

Occasionally, blood transfusions will be given during a severe crisis that could be life-threatening.

Family living Like any chronic illness or disability, sickle cell anaemia is sometimes difficult to come to terms with. A person may feel unable to cope with this inconvenient and painful condition and be frightened of dying at an early age. Support and understanding are needed, particularly during crises. Allowances have to be made.

Education/Training Children with sickle cell anaemia can almost always attend a mainstream school, although they may find it difficult to concentrate when in pain or easily tired and lethargic. It may be necessary to take time off school to attend the hospital centre during crises. Frequently, children get behind in their school work. Co-operation between the school staff, hospital, and family is thus important. Sometimes home or hospital tuition becomes necessary.

If a child or young person complains of severe chest or abdominal pain, headache, neck stiffness, or drowsiness, immediate hospital treatment is usually necessary.

Support agencies The address of the nearest sickle cell centre can be obtained through the Organisation for Sickle Cell Anaemia Research (OSCAR) or the Sickle Cell Society.

Useful literature

- *Sickle cell disease*, Graham Serjeant (Oxford University Press, 1985)
- *Sickle cell disease: a guide for general practitioners, nurses, and other health professionals* (Health Education Council, 1983)
- *Sickle cell disease: a guide for teachers and others caring for children* (Health Education Council, 1983)
- *A handbook on sickle cell disease: a guide for families* (Sickle Cell Society, 1983)
- *Pain in sickle cell disease* (Sickle Cell Society, 1986)
- *Sickle cell anaemia — who cares?* (Runnymede Trust, 1985)

Bone disorders

Arthritis

Introduction   Arthritis is a general term meaning inflammation of a joint or joints. There are approximately 200 different conditions which can cause arthritis. At least eight million people in the UK, i.e. about one-sixth of the total adult population, have some form of arthritis.

Children and young adults can also be affected. Juvenile chronic arthritis affects one child in every 1000 in the UK. One in 20 teenagers and young adults have rheumatoid arthritis or a related condition.

As a result of improved drug therapy, surgery, and replacement therapy, fewer people are now becoming severly disabled by arthritis and rheumatic disease.

Main characteristics   Different forms of arthritis may affect one main joint (monarthritis), a few joints (oligoarthritis), or many joints (polyarthritis).

A distinction can be made between acute and chronic arthritis. With acute athritis, a person experiences a painful hot swollen joint or joints. These symptoms may occur in many infective conditions of a viral or bacterial nature. A chronic arthritic condition, however, has a slow and gradual (insidious) onset and there is often no known cause.

There are two main groups of arthritis: osteoarthritis and rheumatoid arthritis.

i) Osteoarthritis is by far the commonest form, affecting about five million people in the UK. It is largely due to general wear and tear of the joints and thus occurs more frequently with advancing age. It is usually monarticular (involving only one joint) — affecting weight-bearing joints such as the knee, the hip, the ankle, and spinal joints, for example — and does not spread throughout the body.

The smooth cartilage which protects the ends of joint bones wears thin and becomes rough and often a little inflamed. The synovial fluid, an important joint lubricant, increases in quantity and thickens, causing irritation. Spurs of new bone tissue form at the edges of the joint. The result is a swollen joint which may become distorted, stiff, and painful.

ii) Rheumatoid arthritis attacks joints — especially the larger joints of the limbs — and also the tendons and other soft tissues attached to the joints. It is usually polyarticular (involving several joints), but occasionally it starts in one joint and then spreads to others. For most people the condition is usually progressive, and the inflammation is typically severe — the joint becomes swollen, and stiffness and pain or tenderness in motion are common.

Other parts of the body may become affected, causing fever, anaemia, inflammation around the lung (pleurisy), and other complications. The heart and eyes may also be affected.

Nearly one million people in the UK have this condition, which usually starts at about 40 to 50 years of age, although it can occur at any age. It affects three times as many women as men.

Rheumatoid arthritis can be unpredictable and for some it may disappear rapidly, leaving little damage, or over many years may become less and less severe. Some people recover completely without joint disability, others have minor joint abnormalities, and the remainder are moderately to severely affected. One in 10 people with rheumatoid arthritis are severely disabled.

Rheumatoid arthritis in children is called Still's disease. The onset is usually acute, with severe fever and pain in the joints which can come and go before settling in the wrists, hands, knees, elbows, and ankles. The condition is one of remissions and relapses, with the child feeling miserable and unwell when the joints swell again. Sometimes the joints are not involved at the onset and it may be several weeks or months before diagnosis is reached.

Among the more common of the other types of arthritis are ankylosing spondylitis, psoriatic arthritis, and systemic lupus erythematosus. These are dealt with separately at the end of the chapter.

Inheritance pattern In general, arthritis is not inherited but there may be a familial tendency, particularly with rheumatoid arthritis. This means that the condition is slightly more common in some families. Genetic factors may be associated with some less common types of arthritis such as gout, as well in arthritic joints resulting from haemophilia.

Diagnosis Pain is usually the presenting symptom for osteoarthritis, and X-ray changes are characteristic. The synovial fluid has a low cell count.

For rheumatoid arthritis, nodules (subcutaneous over bony promi-
nences) and positive tests for rheumatoid factor in the blood are helpful
in diagnosis. The ESR (erythrocyte sedimentation rate — the rate of
settling of red blood cells in anticoagulated blood, which gives a measure of the increase in any infection) is usually raised, and anaemia is
common. Erosion of the joints may be seen on X-rays, but only after
some time following onset.

In general, the most helpful investigations in order to identify the type
of arthritis include the following:

● A full blood count and an ESR test, which helps distinguish between
  inflammatory and non-inflammatory disease.
● Tests for rheumatoid factor (particularly for rheumatoid arthritis).
● X-rays are important in revealing characteristic appearances of diagnostic value.
● Synovial-fluid examination (synovial biopsy) provides a pointer to
  the intensity of inflammatory changes. However, this is usually
  carried out only when other investigations fail to establish diagnosis.

Treatment   In the 1950s and 1960s, most doctors were unable to offer
much more than regular aspirin to reduce pain and inflammation. Since
then there has been a great increase in interest and in the number of
arthritis and rheumatology specialists in the UK.

It is important to keep the joints mobile and the muscles in good
shape. Drug therapy and physical therapy need to be combined with
rest. Most treatments are geared to reducing pain and inflammation.

Sometimes drugs are injected directly into the joints. In rheumatoid
arthritis, gold compounds, d-penicillamine, or corticosteroids may be
used. Physiotherapy includes the use of heat and remedial bath
treatment.

The lives of many people are transformed by a wide range of advanced
operations, including replacement joints for the hip, knee, wrist, finger,
etc. However, surgery is usually considered only after drug treatment has
been tried for some time.

Diet and exercise   Although there are many ideas concerning diet, in
general there is no evidence to suggest that it may be a prime factor in
control. Nevertheless, it is helpful if diets are high in protein and calcium, and vitamin supplements are sometimes recommended. Being
overweight (obesity) can place undue stress on uncomfortable joints.

Regular rest periods throughout the day help to conserve energy, but it
is important not to sit too long in one position. Excess exercise in general
can aggravate joint deterioration.

Family living   For people with rheumatoid arthritis, painful flare-ups can occur frequently and suddenly, yet at other times there may be weeks, months, or even years when the condition is not so troublesome. In general, people with arthritis suffer different degrees of discomfort. For some it may only be painful to walk upstairs, but for others the constant pain, day and night, despite drug therapy, can be very wearing.

Depression itself usually lowers the pain threshold, and thus it is crucial for people to try to continue activities and develop new interests.

Support from family and friends in alleviating depression, irritability, frustration, and loneliness is important. The help of family members may be constantly needed in both a physical and emotional sense, and this can be draining and upsetting for them.

Rheumatoid arthritis tends to improve during pregnancy, but, for some women with arthritis, stiff hip joints may mean that a Caesarean operation is more appropriate.

People learn to reduce pressure on affected joints by lifting, pushing, etc. using stronger joints. Labour-saving devices are essential in the home. Every routine job takes twice as long, and many people feel frustrated at not being able to perform tasks as effectively as they once could.

For those younger people affected, modern drug therapy, careful management, and support can help to achieve independence. In many cases the difference between coping with the condition or not means being able to obtain the right kind of assistance — whether information or financial help — encouragement and practical support from family, friends, and professionals, together with a positive attitude towards life and disability.

Mobility For about 10% of people with arthritis, the condition is completely disabling.

Aids such as powered wheelchairs for use in and out of the home, lifting devices to enable the person to get in and out of a car, plus several modifications to cars for easy driving, can be crucial in allowing a person to maintain a reasonable degree of independence. The Disabled Drivers Association can give some guidance.

Employment Employers, like the general public, have not always realised that medical progress has meant that people with arthritis can successfully undertake full employment. Although there may be increasing physical limitations, the need for long periods off work due to illness is now less likely.

Most people with osteoarthritis are able to continue working, but certain aids and adaptations may be necessary. The occupational therapist can advise employers on minor adaptations and equipment.

Aids and benefits There is a vast range of practical aids which can assist in the home and work situations. Some aid independent living, and other adaptations and equipment help carers to assist more effectively. Advice concerning aids and adaptations can be sought from the occupational therapist.

Benefits which may be appropriate include mobility allowance, invalid care allowance, and attendance allowance. Further information can be obtained from the DHSS.

Support agencies   Arthritis Care, in association with the Lady Hoare Trust, is the only national welfare organisation concerned with arthritis in the UK. Formerly known as The British Rheumatism and Arthritis Association, it aims to provide information, advice, and practical aid and to improve facilities on a social and welfare level.

There are a network of branches throughout the country and a home visiting service which can provide therapeutic work at home for those who are handicapped. A regular newspaper, general literature, and information concerning holiday centres and residential homes are available. Arthritis Care itself provides several holiday centres, self-catering holiday units, and a residential home.

An under-35 group provides social and welfare support for young people with arthritis. Regional groups are organised to provide friendship and support and to highlight the problems of arthritis in the young. A bimonthly magazine, *In contact*, is available.

The Lady Hoare Trust has 24 medical social workers covering the whole of the UK and offers a personal visiting service to all young people up to the age of 17 years. Advice on aids, education, housing, finances, etc. can be provided.

The Arthritis and Rheumatism Council is mainly concerned with raising funds for research. It publishes a number of handbooks for people with arthritis.

The Disabled Living Foundation is an important source of advice and information on aids and equipment after individual advice has been taken from the occupational therapist.

Useful literature

- *Arthritis and rheumatism: the facts*, J.T. Scott (Oxford University Press, 1980)
- Arthritis Care publishes a range of leaflets.

Ankylosing spondylitis

This condition often starts with pain and stiffness in the lower back and can affect joints of the hip and knee. Bone grows out from both sides of some, or all, of the 24 vertebrae in the spine, and there can be serious difficulty with movement. It is sometimes called 'poker-back'.

The early painful stages can be relieved by treatment with drugs, spinal exercises, and physiotherapy. For some people the disorder manifests itself only in aches and pains, but difficulty in stooping and bending is also common.

This condition may run in families, and it has been discovered that about 95% of people with this condition have the tissue type HLA B27, which is found in only about 7% of the population. The chances of passing the condition on to a child is in the region of 1 in 50.

The National Ankylosing Spondylitis Society provides support and advice to families. It publishes a biannual newsletter, and information on special exercises is available on tape.

Psoriatic arthritis

This condition is similar to rheumatoid arthritis but usually affects fewer joints and is generally milder. Joints near the fingertips are commonly affected, and the fingernails may become pitted or severely damaged.

Treatment is given in the same way as for rheumatoid arthritis.

The Psoriasis Association sponsors research and provides support and advice.

Systemic lupus erythematosus

This condition is characterised by skin rashes on various parts of the body, usually accompanied by inflammation of the joints. Other symptoms include kidney disease, heart disease, neurological disorders, hair loss, pregnancy problems, etc. Systemic lupus erythematosus (SLE) is now known to be a more common rheumatic condition than previously thought and usually affects people under the age of 40 years.

SLE is nine times more common in women than in men, and children may also be affected. The incidence in women is 1 per 2000, and most are of child-bearing age.

Over 95% of people with SLE have joint problems although, unlike rheumatoid arthritis, it rarely causes damage to bones. The extent of disability varies, but drug treatments may help control the condition, and with careful management most people can expect a normal lifespan.

The Lupus Group is basically a self-help group for people with SLE. A contact scheme with regional support groups exists throughout the UK. The group is part of Arthritis Care.

Brittle bone disease

Introduction   Brittle bone disease (osteogenesis imperfecta) is thought to be not a single condition but a combination of at least seven distinct disorders, all caused by inborn abnormalities in the fundamental structure of the protein part of the bone. It is not caused by lack of calcium and is quite distinct from the bone fragility seen in older women (osteoporosis).

About 2500 people in Britain have brittle bone disease.

Main characteristics   The severity of the disorder varies greatly. Some infants with brittle bones are born with fractures. Others have their first injury soon after birth or when first attempting to walk.

Fractures happen with frightening simplicity, for example during nappy-changing or while turning over in bed, closing a door, or even switching off the television. Some children have as many as 50 to 100 fractures in childhood, with milder cases having between 10 and 50.

In very severe cases many more fractures occur. Many of these children are very short in statute and spend life permanently in a wheelchair.

Healing of fractures occurs readily, but if a particular bone suffers numerous fractures it may result in permanent deformities. Very rarely, callus formation (part of the normal healing process) may cause severe disability.

Other symptoms may include a bluish colour in the whites of the eyes, and sometimes the head is flattened with bulging at the side, giving a characteristic appearance. Deafness may occur in later life. Loose-jointedness may be a problem for some people.

Inheritance   In some cases, mostly where the disorder is mild, there is evidence of inheritance from one generation to another. In almost all severe cases, there is no known family history.

Treatment   No effective drug therapy is known, but much can be done with orthopaedic surgery. Each fracture has to be treated carefully, to prevent the bones healing with deformity.

A small proportion of affected children benefit from wearing a 'space suit' (a pair of trouser with inflatable supports) which allows a child to stand.

Family living   Parents have a difficult task trying to prevent their child from taking risks but at the same time trying not to be overprotective.

Throughout childhood, each child is faced with a constant fear of painful bone fractures. Each fracture may necessitate several weeks in traction in hospital or in plaster at home. Either prospect means a long period of monotony, boredom, and restriction which seems like an eternity to a small child.

Those children who are permanently wheelchair-bound experience acute frustration and may not be able to participate in the usual range of children's activities.

Mobility Children with the most severe types of brittle bone disease may never be able to stand or walk, but the specially designed equipment which is now available may enable them to enjoy increased mobility and independence.

Education There are no special schools catering specifically for children with brittle bones, but even children who are severely affected can usually be educated in mainstream primary and secondary schools. A good standard of education is important, as these children need the right opportunities to become independent. The condition does not affect intelligence.

Some children have such weakness in their fingers that a specially adapted typewriter can make all the difference to their progress in education.

The Brittle Bone Society issues a special leaflet of information for teachers.

Employment Many people with a brittle bone disability, particularly with the milder varieties of the disorder, have no difficulty in obtaining employment. An appreciable proportion of severely affected adults are employed in a variety of non-manual occupations.

Aids and benefits Equipment much needed by children with brittle bones includes powered wheelchairs, special typewriters, adapted toys, and bathroom aids. These are often not available through the National Health Service or from social services departments. It is not always appreciated that children as young as four years can cope with a powered chair.

Children with brittle bones are generally intelligent and, given the right education and equipment, many can anticipate an independent and self-supporting adult life.

The costs of parents frequently visiting their child in hospital can be severe. Appropriate benefits include attendance allowance and mobility allowance. Family Fund may be particularly helpful.

Support agencies The Brittle Bone Society was established in 1972. It aims to promote research into brittle bones and to provide practical support, advice, and encouragement to families. A regular newsletter offers practical advice, and a contact network offers support between families. Holiday facilities are provided.

The Society has part-time occupational therapists who visit children in their homes to ensure that they get the equipment most suited to their needs. Special aids can in some cases be funded by the Society.

Useful literature

The Brittle Bone Society provides a comprehensive range of leaflets.

Paget's disease

Introduction　Sir James Paget first described Paget's disease (PD) over one hundred years ago, but early Saxon burials contain evidence of deformities such as those found in PD.

This condition is more common with advancing age and involves a thickening and deformity in the structure of the bone. Such changes may be confined to one bone or may involve many bones in different part of the body. For a few people it may be so severe that in the later stages they may be bedridden.

Although there are about 2500 known cases in the UK, it is suggested that there may be well over this number.

Main characteristics　Symptoms vary widely but may include a thickening of some bones, yet others go paper thin, and a reduction in height. Hearing impairment is common, and visual impairment may also develop. Pressure behind the eyes and a type of glaucoma (an eye condition which results in loss of vision) may be experienced, but these are less common.

Affected bones are more likely to fracture than unaffected bones, and they are less likely to heal as well or as quickly.

Causes　There is no known cause, but research is currently considering several possibilities, including the possibility that the condition may lie dormant from a childhood illness and be triggered off later by some other cause, or that there may be a link with allergies affecting the immunity system (associated with a family pet etc., for example).

It is now thought that there is a juvenile type of this disorder.

Inheritance pattern　Paget's disease is sometimes hereditary.

Diagnosis   PD may frequently be mistaken for other conditions such as lumbago, sciatica, fibrositis, etc., as symptoms in the early stages may be severe backache and sometimes chest pains. X-rays generally help diagnosis.

Treatment   For many people, treatment involves drug therapy which aids pain relief and acts directly on the bone. Some do not require regular treatment other than analgesics (painkillers). A nasal drug has recently been used, and several other drugs are undergoing research.

Treatment is given on an out-patient basis. Some respond well, but not all.

Family living   Due to the little information and understanding of this relatively uncommon condition, families often feel isolated and unsupported. When treatment is not considered appropriate and there is therefore no contact with professionals, the person affected by Paget's disease may feel confused and remain conscious of his or her deteriorating condition.

Falls, injuries, and accidents are likely to cause fractures and hasten the crippling effects of the disease.

Pain becomes a major element in life, although only a few people may experience severe discomfort. Anxiety concerning uncertainties, misunderstandings, and frustrations — particularly in relation to prognosis — may itself decrease pain tolerance and the family's ability to cope.

Adapting to a change in lifestyle as the condition slowly progresses is important.

Mobility   Mobility may be seriously affected in the later stages.

Employment   Where symptoms persist, early retirement may be appropriate.

Support agencies   The National Association for the Relief of Paget's Disease was formed in 1973. It provides information to members and sponsors research.

Useful literature

● *Paget's atlas* (Armour Pharmaceutical Co.)

Chest/heart disorders

Asthma

Introduction   Asthma is a common disorder causing reversible airways obstruction. It can affect both children and adults. It is estimated that one child in ten will have asthma. The bronchial airways (breathing tubes) are oversensitive and react to various provoking factors by contracting suddenly into an involuntary spasm. Breathing becomes difficult and rapid in an effort to obtain more oxygen and produces an audible wheeze. If the attack is severe, there is a sensation of choking which can be a frightening experience. In between these attacks, breathing is normal.

Main characteristics   Most children with asthma have allergies to certain substances (allergens) and contact with them produces an attack. However, wheezing may be precipitated by other factors — such as emotional upsets, infection, air pollution, vigorous exercise, changes in the weather, etc. — but these are not primary causes of the condition.

An acute attack may last for only a few minutes, but it is not uncommon for the symptoms to persist for several hours or longer, especially if effective treatment is not given in good time.

Some children with asthma eventually grow out of it, or at least the condition becomes less troublesome.

Causes   Asthma is an inborn constitutional disorder and is not an infectious disease. There are two main types:

i) Allergic asthma (which is the commonest form in children) affects people who are abnormally sensitive to common substances such as grass pollen, house dust, house mites, feathers, animal hair, etc. Allergy to food is less common. Allergic asthma occurs more often in boys than in girls and its incidence is increasing.

ii) A second type of asthma begins in adulthood and is not usually associated with allergies. There may be additional nasal symptoms such as catarrh, sinusitis, etc.

Inheritance pattern There is a tendency for asthma and related conditions such as hay fever, eczema, and skin allergies to run in families.

Diagnosis Many infants wheeze occasionally, but this is usually related to a chest infection. Bronchitis may be diagnosed initially. In general, most asthmatic children begin wheezing in their first two years. Skin tests (usually on those over the age of four years) can help to identify the suspected allergen. A more recently developed test is able to detect the allergic antibodies in the blood. This radio-allergosorbent test can be done in most hospitals. The result is expressed as an IgE level.

Treatment The usual form of treatment is with bronchodilator drugs which relax the spasm of the bronchial tubes. These may be given in tablet form, as a linctus, or via a pocket inhaler. During a severe attack, an injection may be needed.

For very severe asthma, the preferred treatment is with the use of steroids. These usually produce dramatic improvement within 24 to 48 hours. Sometimes a short course is needed; sometimes only a maintenance dose to keep the asthma under control. Steroids can be taken by means of a pocket inhaler, therefore only a small dose is required. This minimises the risk of side-effects.

As wells as steroids, modern drugs which help to prevent attacks include Intal (cromolyn sodium). This has been particularly effective for about 60% of children with asthma. Physiotherapy also forms a basic part of treatment, and special breathing exercises may be used during an attack to help control.

Asthma attacks can to some extent be prevented by avoiding the allergen. Asthma can also be helped by desensitisation, which involves building up resistance to an allergen by injecting, over a period, gradually increasing doses of the allergen.

It is also important to start symptomatic treatment with bronchodilators at the very onset of an attack. Parents are often able to predict when their child is likely to have an attack. Attacks can vary in severity, thus, if wheezing persists and becomes worse despite treatment, it is vital that the GP is called.

It is important to accurately identify the offending allergic factors, as prevention is a vital part of treatment.

Diet and exercise Regular exercise is important, and so is participating in usual activities. For some children, but less commonly in adults, asthma may be brought on by vigorous exercise such as running. However Intal, taken beforehand, can be helpful and allow the child to participate in sports.

Family living   For children with asthma it is usually necessary to reduce the provoking allergens. By far the most common allergy in children with asthma is to domestic house dust and, in particular, the house-dust mite. The bedroom is particularly likely to contain both of these. They can be reduced by using lino instead of carpets and man-made fibres for blankets, mattresses, etc. Bedclothes need to be laundered frequently. The use of a vacuum cleaner is most effective in preventing dust in the air.

In addition, it is useful to remove possible causes in order to identify the allergen — for example the family pet, and certain foods such as egg and milk.

The child with asthma needs to be encouraged to participate in life alongside his or her contempories. This is understandably difficult for those parents who feel that their child needs extra protection and may see him or her as delicate. It is equally important that parents do not try to harden their child by withholding drugs in an effort to increase independence.

Continued contact with the GP can provide the necessary support and reassurance which most families need.

Education   Attendance in mainstream schools is usually encouraged. For those children who find their disability a great handicap or whose condition is particularly severe, it may be useful to consider specialised schooling.

The Invalid Children's Aid Association (ICAA) runs a school for children with chronic asthma: Pilgrims School in East Sussex which caters for 12- to 16-year-olds from all over the country. Children who attend the school are usually those who have required long periods of hospitalisation in the past. Supportive nursing physiotherapy is provided, and the school aims to encourage confidence and independence.

Further education/Employment   Many children, especially boys, tend to grow out of their asthma, but for others the symptoms continue into adult life. Some people find that they experience repeated chest infections throughout life even though severe asthma attacks have ceased. These factors may have a bearing on further education and choice of employment.

Those asthmatic children who have missed a great deal of school in their early years may need to spend further time in colleges to improve their level of education before making career choices.

Adults with asthma may be limited in their choice of employment due to the factors which exacerbate their condition and bring on asthmatic attacks.

Aids and benefits In some cases, the attendance allowance may be relevant.

Support agencies The Chest, Heart and Stroke Association works for the prevention of asthma and to help those with this condition. It carries out a programme of health education, research, welfare, and counselling.

The Asthma Society provides assistance to people with asthma and their families and organises local support branches throughout the UK. Booklets concerning asthma and its treatment are available for families and professionals.

Useful literature

- Asthma Society leaflets include:

  Asthma and allergy
  Coming to terms with asthma
  Asthma at school
  Understanding asthma
  How to cope with asthma attack

- *Asthma: the facts*, Donald Lane and Anthony Storr (Oxford University Press, 1979)
- *Life with asthma*, H. Wykeham Balme (Family Doctor Publications, 1982)
- *The child with asthma*, Kate Rackham (Invalid Children's Aid Association, 1976)

Heart disease

Introduction Heart disease is a general term which describes any abnormal condition of the heart. It includes irregular functioning of the heart, as well as diseases of the coronary arteries, heart valves, and heart muscle.

In the Western world, coronary heart disease is of major concern, especially to middle-aged people. This is a degenerative condition in

130 Understanding disability

which the coronary arteries supplying the blood (and thus oxygen) to the heart muscle become narrowed and obstructed. Following a coronary heart attack (coronary thrombosis — blockage of the blood supply by a blood clot), most people recover as the heart muscle heals.

Coronary heart disease may give rise to angina, in which a person experiences pain in the chest and sometimes in the arms, neck, and back on exercise or occasionally at rest. This is due to a temporary impairment of the blood supply to the heart muscle.

Congenital heart disease is an abnormality of the heart which has been present since birth. It occurs in about 8 of every 1000 children born alive. About one-third of these children have only mild heart abnormalities and never require any treatment. Some children are born with heart defects such as valve abnormalities or 'holes in the heart'.

Valvular disease may follow rheumatic fever.

Heart muscle disease may be due to a variety of causes, which include viral infections and alcohol abuse. It is also often associated with other medical conditions.

Inheritance pattern   The risk of another child with congenital heart disease being born to parents of a child with the condition is about 1 in 50.

Some families may experience a higher than usual incidence of coronary heart disease. Families where heart disease has occurred in several generations should therefore be encouraged to reduce risk factors.

Diagnosis   A major symptom of congenital heart disease in a newborn child is a bluish complexion (cyanosis). Also, the baby may pant during feeding or seem difficult to feed. Respiratory difficulties, or sometimes a chronic cough, and weariness may also be characteristic of the condition. Recurrent respiratory infections are more liable to occur in a baby with congenital heart disease.

If a heart murmur has been heard, the baby is usually kept under observation as it is necessary to distinguish between an 'innocent' (insignificant) and an 'organic' (significant) murmur.

At any age when a heart condition is suspected, an X-ray of the heart and an electrocardiogram are usual. If necessary, an echocardiogram (scan of the heart) is an additional test. In some babies and children, a heart catheterisation test (inserting a tube into the heart) is helpful to obtain more precise information.

Retarded growth may be the result of growing tissues receiving insufficient blood, and thus the possibility of congenital heart damage needs to be considered in infants who fail to thrive.

Treatment   Drug therapy is available to cure or lessen many forms of heart disease. Surgery can be dramatic in the correction of abnormalities of the heart valves and of congenital defects.

Some parents or relatives may be distressed by the sight of the support equipment necessary following an operation. It is important for families to discuss the implications of a particular operation with medical staff and to gain some explanation and understanding of what is involved.

Diet and exercise   People who have had coronary heart disease need to increase their physical activity but avoid excessive exercise and competitive sports. Smoking must be avoided, and weight should be controlled by a suitable diet. Attention should be given to reducing fats in the diet, especially saturated (i.e. animal) fats. This regime is appropriate for all who wish to minimise the risk of coronary heart disease.

Children will usually discover the limits of their physical capacity, adjusting the level of activity accordingly.

Family living   A change in lifestyle may be necessary for someone with heart disease. In some cases a person may need a home help or a community or district nurse to assist with medication. The domiciliary occupational therapist from the social services department can advise on major adaptations to the home when relevant.

For young children with congenital heart disease, the risk of infection is greater than average and thus a young baby needs to be kept away from crowded places. In general, such children are rarely sent to schools for children with special needs, and restrictions on activity etc. should be kept to a minimum to avoid their feeling that they are different from their friends.

Support agencies   The Chest, Heart and Stroke Association provides a comprehensive range of literature to families and professionals. The aims of this organisation place a strong emphasis on preventive work. The British Heart Foundation, the heart research charity, provides helpful fact-sheets for parents and families and information concerning a wide range of support groups.

Useful literature

- CHSA leaflets include *Heart disease – twenty questions and answers*.
- The British Heart Foundation offers a wide range of leaflets, including *Back to normal (following a heart attack), Heart surgery for adults, Congenital heart disease, Modern heart medicines, The heart and its problems,* and *Valvular heart disease.*
- *Coronary heart disease: the facts*, J.P Shillingford (Oxford University Press, 1981)
- *Beat heart disease*, Risteard Mulcahy (Martin Dunitz, 1979)

Skin disorders

Eczema

Introduction Eczema is an itchy, sore, and often disfiguring skin condition affecting millions of people to some degree. It is most common in children, but can occur at any age. It is not infectious.

Main characteristics There are at least 14 different types of eczema. These have various causes, including exposure of the skin to irritants such as detergents, wool, etc.; particular chemicals; bacterial and fungal infections; sun exposure; and drug ingestion.

- Lichen simplex is where thickened pigmented patches become worse during stress.
- Atopic eczema is part of the asthma/hay-fever syndrome and the commonest form is infantile eczema. The rash affects the elbows, wrists, knee flexures, etc.
- Seborrhoeic eczema may start as cradle cap (dermatitis of the scalp) and move to the face, ears, and neck. Patches also may be found on the chest, back, groin, and underarms. This type usually clears spontaneously after a few months, but can continue in adulthood.
- Pompholyx is an acute blistering type of eczema, mainly affecting the palms of the hands and the soles of the feet. Secondary infection is common.

Inheritance pattern Infantile eczema is the most common form and tends to run in families. A relative may have asthma or hay fever, which are linked to eczema.

Diagnosis Eczema usually starts with patches of dry itchy skin which may be behind the ears and knees, in the body creases at elbows and neck, on the face and trunk, or in the scalp. When severe, the skin may be red, raw, weeping, or crusted and can become infected.

It is important to obtain diagnosis of the type of eczema by the family doctor or specialist.

Infantile eczema (atopic eczema) is fairly common, but for some people this type of eczema can come and go throughout life.

Treatment Some substances can cause eczema to flare up simply by contact with the skin, but others need to get into the body before they have any effect.

Certain creams inhibit the allergic response. In addition, creams may help itching and inflammation. Antihistamine in liquid or tablet form is used. Some steroid drugs have been effective in the treatment of eczema.

The herpes-simplex (cold sore) virus is a particular danger to the person with eczema as it causes widespread infection of the rash.

Diet and exercise Controversy still centres around the connections between eczema and diet, but some substances — notably additives and preservatives used in frozen, packaged, and tinned foods — do seem to have a drastic effect on certain people. Milk, eggs, and cheese are also foods which many people find cause an allergic reaction.

Family living Many children have experienced severe eczema from the age of only a few months and make regular visits to the doctor for most of their childhood. In some situations, care as a hospital in-patient is necessary.

Babies with eczema may be irritable and restless and sleep badly. Some may suffer from colic and vomiting or may be very active and lively. It is important for parents to comfort and cuddle their child, as this condition can be very sore and distressing.

Parents need to be aware when a child with eczema is being teased and ridiculed by other children. Intervention may be necessary. As a teenager, embarrassment is made worse by the need to feel attractive to the opposite sex.

In general, plenty of reassurance is needed, as this condition can be constantly uncomfortable and may only seem to improve for short periods in adulthood.

People with eczema and their families have to cope with the unpleasant physical symptoms together with the social, emotional, and practical problems. Due largely to the lack of information and to mis-understandings by the general public, people with eczema may feel rejected and may even isolate themselves from the community.

Education School staff need to be kept informed about the effects that eczema and its treatment may have on a child. How a child's teacher handles the problems will have far-reaching effects on the child's condition and general behaviour at home as well as at school.

Antihistamine may make the child sleepy, and irritation may disturb concentration. It is helpful if children have creams for use as soap and to ease irritation while at school.

In the past, some children with eczema have been sent to schools for the delicate, but nowadays such children usually attend mainstream schools, with a few benefiting from residential care.

The soreness and stiffness of limbs may make children miserable, and this sometimes leads to behaviour problems. Frequent days off school may be needed because the eczema is infected or simply has become very severe. There may be additional problems of asthma or hay fever and a general lowered resistance to common illnesses.

On some days, a child with eczema may find it difficult to walk, smile, or even hold a pencil. On other days, the problems may not be evident.

It may be possible to get dispensation from examination boards on medical grounds if the eczema flares up. Dictating facilities may be allowed.

Employment   Career choice can be limited, as certain jobs are inadvisable for people with eczema.

Support agencies   The National Eczema Society has a number of local support and information groups. A comprehensive range of literature is available, including information packs for adults and for children.

The Hyperactive Children's Support Group provides information about diet.

Useful literature

Eczema and dermatitis, Rona Mackie (Martin Dunitz, 1983)
Learning to live with skin disorders, Christine Orton (Souvenir Press, 1981)
Your child with eczema, David Atherton (William Heinemann Medical Books, 1984)

Psoriasis

Introduction   Psoriasis is a common skin condition which at some time and to a varying extent affects over a million people in the UK.

The condition affects men and women equally and may appear at any age. However the most frequent occurrence is at between 14 and 45 years of age, notably during adolescence, pregnancy, and the menopause, although it may also disappear at those times.

Main characteristics Psoriasis is a condition which appears as raised red patches of skin covered with silvery scales. It can occur on any part of the body, although the knees, elbows, and scalp are the usual sites. There is often accompanying irritation.

Psoriasis is not contagious, nor is it caused by poor standards of hygiene.

There can be considerable variations in intensity, from a few patches to a widespread and serious eruption. It is known as a waxing and waning condition.

Rare forms which can produce serious symptoms may need intensive medical and nursing care.

About 6% of people with psoriasis develop a specific type of psoriatic arthritis which is generally a mild affliction of the joints at the tips of the fingers and in the toes and occasionally lumbar joints.

Causes/Inheritance pattern The basic cause of psoriasis is not known. Hereditary factors are thought to play an important part, although the actual pattern of inheritance is not clear. It is suggested that a genetic tendency may be triggered off by injury, throat infection, certain drugs, and both physical and emotional stress.

Treatment A great variety of treatments exists, but some are cosmetically unacceptable or difficult to use while others may in themselves be toxic or have side-effects.

Approximately one-third of people with psoriasis lose the condition naturally for long periods of time or even entirely.

There is no known cure for this condition at present.

Family living Widespread ignorance as to the nature of psoriasis and the reactions and attitudes of others towards a person with psoriasis may lead to withdrawal from society and to feelings of isolation, depression, and defensive shyness.

The anger and frustration of coming to terms with a chronic condition such as psoriasis may result in negative attitudes to both carers and the professionals involved.

Support agencies The Psoriasis Association provides information concerning this condition and aims to increase public acceptance and understanding. It is a self-help organisation offering support and mutual aid to all those who have psoriasis and their families through local groups and branches.

Useful literature

- *Continuing care: management of chronic disease*, John Hasler and Theo Schofield (Oxford University Press, 1984)
- *Practical problems in dermatology*, Ronald Marks (Martin Dunitz, 1983)
- *Psoriasis: a guide to one of the commonest skin disorders*, Ronald Marks (Martin Dunitz, 1981)

Sensory handicaps

Hearing impairment

Introduction It is suggested that up to ten million people in the UK have some difficulty with hearing. That is an incidence of 1 in 5. Many of these people also have additional disabilities. In reality, few people will not experience some hearing loss in their lifetime.

Despite improved primary health care, hearing problems among the aged are as prevalent as ever. Added to those problems that are simply age-induced are those that are caused by the general increase in noise levels.

Main characteristics The outer ear and middle ear are responsible for conducting sound through the eardrum and the ossicles to the oval window (see the diagram below). Any interruption to this process is called 'conductive' deafness.

The cochlea is a sense organ of hearing and is connected to the brain by the auditory nerve. Damage to the cochlea causes nerve deafness, which is also called 'sensory—neural' deafness or 'perceptive' deafness.

'Recruitment' is a problem commonly associated with nerve deafness: although quiet sounds cannot be heard, loud sounds appear louder and very loud sounds can be painful. Shouting and too much amplification produce distortion and make speech more difficult to understand.

Tinnitus is experienced by two out of three people with a hearing loss. Noises in the head such as ringing, whistling, etc., which can be loud and distressing, are experienced. Mostly this is due to tiny abnormalities in the cochlea or the auditory nerve. The condition cannot be surgically treated. Drug therapy does not always alleviate symptoms, but a tinnitus masker (worn in the ear) is helpful to cover up noises in the head.

Vertigo or giddiness may be present in nerve deafness, as the cochlea is linked to the organs of balance.

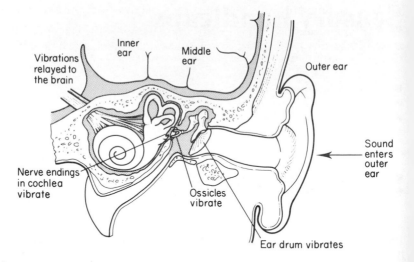

Fig. 6 Sound passes through the ear and the vibrations are interpreted by the brain.

Manière's disease, in which there is an increase in fluid pressure in the inner ear, can sometimes be helped by surgery.

Otosclerosis is a hereditary condition involving severe progressive hearing loss as the stirrup within the ear becomes fixed to the oval window by an abnormal growth of bone. It can be relieved by operation.

Causes   A major distinction can be made between those people whose hearing impairment occurred during the pre-lingual period (congenital and neonatal impairment) and thus before the child had learnt to appreciate sound and those people whose hearing became impaired during the post-lingual period. In the latter case, knowledge, vocabulary, and experience of speaking are retained.

Causes of early hearing impairment include the following:

● Malformation of the cochlear nerve. Some varieties of congenital nerve deafness are inherited.

● Congenital defects or absence of the outer, middle, and inner ear occasionally occur, in thalidomide children for example.

● Maternal rubella (German measles) occurring during the first three months of pregnancy is likely to cause damage to the child's cochlea. The risk of hearing impairment is about 30%. Immunisation against rubella is thus important.

● Head injury at birth and asphyxia may also result in hearing impairment.

Late or acquired hearing impairment may be caused by the following:

- A common cause is otitis media (inflammation of the ear), particularly secretory otitis media or 'glue ear' where there is a chronic discharge of fluid. The damage can be greater if the condition is allowed to continue or be recurrent.
- Meningitis or encephalitis may lead to hearing impairment.
- It can be a complication of mumps.
- Traumatic injury may result in some part of the auditory pathway being damaged or destroyed. For example, it has been estimated that two million workers in the UK are exposed to noise levels above the maximum regarded as safe by the Health and Safety Executive.
- Toxic action of certain drugs, such as Streptomycin.
- Blockage of the external auditory meatus by wax or a foreign body is a simple cause of hearing problems but one which can usually be remedied.

Diagnosis Advances in technology have led to improved diagnosis, assessment, and rehabilitation. Hearing detection in premature babies and new more efficient hearing tests are being developed. For example, the auditory-response cradle can detect deafness in babies of two or three days old.

Initially parents may suspect a hearing difficulty or realise that there is something wrong with their child's response to the world and seek medical advice. Acquired partial loss of hearing is more difficult to appreciate.

Regular checks by the health clinic are important, but there may be a delay in diagnosing hearing problems in childhood until the difficulties become serious. A survey by the National Deaf Children's Society suggested that almost half of those children with hearing loss had not been detected when screened as babies.

Assistance to parents in how they may best help their child in the early learning years is vital. Total deafness is unusual, but continuous assessment is important for the first two years at least.

Treatment Conductive deafness can often be relieved: accumulations of wax in the outer ear canal can be removed; infections can be treated in the eardrum and middle-ear ossicles; perforation of the eardrum can be grafted; and lost or destroyed ossicles can sometimes be replaced or repositioned. Otosclerosis can be relieved by operation.

Nerve deafness can rarely be treated medically or surgically. However, a cochlear implant has recently become available.

It is vital that hearing loss is treated as early as possible. Unfortunately, long waiting lists can mean delays in seeing the hospital audiologist. People are often unwilling to admit to hearing problems as they fear ridicule, embarrassment, or being thought stupid. There may also be a difficulty in coming to terms with acquired deafness if this is seen as a sign of getting old!

There are at least twenty different professional groups which should be involved in care, treatment, and multidisciplinary research. However, services and assessment facilities can vary greatly from one part of the country to another.

Family living   Deafness is a hidden handicap and one that is often misunderstood. The way in which the disability affects people is related to the time when the hearing loss became evident — thus there are different kinds of limitations for the partially hearing, the post-lingually deaf, the born deaf, and those elderly people with acquired hearing loss.

Hearing impairment often leads to isolation which can be frustrating and bewildering. Loneliness may be a major problem and may be caused initially by communication problems.

Difficulty in talking with friends, family, colleagues, or people in shops can become disheartening and frustrating. Both sides may reduce contact because it is that much more demanding and wearing. Some hearing people can become frustrated, impatient, and embarrassed — even shouting unnecessarily. Patience and understanding is thus needed to make communication enjoyable on both sides.

Many people choose to have social contact with others who have a hearing disability and can feel more relaxed using sign language. However, it is important that people feel able to be integrated into the hearing community at home, at work, in leisure pursuits, etc.

Although there may be difficulties to start with — for example, in understanding speech which may not be too clear — the practice of lip-reading can help develop confidence, and with time both parties can find that conversation is not quite so demanding after all. However, use of language may be limited, and some deaf people's speech may be understood only by close family and their teacher. Thus for some people lip-reading may never be successful, but emphasis can be usefully placed on non-verbal communication (generally known as 'people reading').

Everyday sound levels that are accepted by the hearing world can prove to be a major problem to the person with a hearing impairment. Station announcements, telephone bells, doorbells, alarms, etc. may be inaudible. It may not be possible to enjoy TV, radio, theatre, cinema, meetings, music, etc. The telephone has become an integral part of our lives and, although there are adaptations available, only a small number of hearing-impaired people have these.

The unpleasant continuous noises in the head due to tinnitus can contribute to further frustrations.

Difficulties that arise from hearing impairment are very subjective, and sympathetic understanding together with positive help from the community at large are needed. Residential homes for the profoundly deaf are provided by some voluntary organisations.

Education At one time, it was thought beneficial for a young child with severe hearing impairment to attend residential school from a very early age. The number requiring special educational treatment has fallen nationally, and, notably since the Education Act 1981, many more children with hearing impairments now attend local schools. These may be mainstream schools or, often where there are additional disabilities, schools for children with special needs.

To obtain the maximum benefit from early learning experience in the family environment, with its psychological advantages, adequate community-care back-up is required, as within the hearing world.

Teachers in all schools need to take into consideration that most children will experience hearing loss at some time. The Royal National Institute for the Deaf (RNID) found that 20% of five-year-olds have hearing difficulties caused by middle-ear infections, often related to colds. If a hearing impairment is suspected, the school doctor needs to be informed. Teachers can offer support by being aware of the difficulties. Close liaison with peripatetic teachers of the deaf is important. Radio aids to hearing, which link the teacher's voice to the child wherever the teacher is standing, may be available.

For those children with early hearing impairment, the use of language can be limited. Difficulty in thinking in abstract terms, double meanings, etc. continue to isolate the child from his or her contempories and prevent the same kind of progress in school. However this is only one explanation of the problems encountered with learning in school, as multiple learning difficulties may be interpreted in different ways.

Children with problems, including emotional problems, may experience learning difficulties which require specialist attention. With specialist teaching, children can learn to speak.

The present emphasis is on using all aids to communication together, rather than confining a person's skill to one type of communication only.

Further education and training Some people with severe hearing impairment but with the potential to take higher education or training courses may need the support of interpreters able to communicate manually or take notes for them. Assistance from both statutory and voluntary schemes may be available, although these kinds of service are often in short supply.

Certain voluntary organisations, such as the RNID, provide hostel provision near to their specialist training and rehabilitation centres.

Employment   Training opportunities are vital if people with hearing impairment are to compete equitably with hearing people. Links with the disabled resettlement officer and the school careers officer, as well as with employers, are of great importance.

There are still misconceptions within society about the kinds of jobs that people with a hearing disability may be able to do. With the range of technical aids now available, the career choice is no longer strictly limited.

Aids and benefits   It is often thought that a hearing aid will restore normal hearing. For most people it is a valuable means of improving communication, but the sound invariably remains unclear. Hearing aids have become small and efficient and may be worn on the body or at ear-level.

Examples of other aids include flashing alarm clocks, television adaptors, light-operating 'doorbells', devices to attach to the phone (including the inductive coupler in all public or emergency phones), and installations in rooms (such as loop systems in public halls). New technology and the microchip bring visual phones, teletext, and further innovations yet to be developed.

Hearing aids alone can be of limited value, but simultaneous lip-reading and observation of hand gestures may provide vital cues for understanding. Lip-reading is a difficult skill and requires constant concentration on the part of the lip-reader. Classes are run in many parts of the country, not only for the hard of hearing but also for their friends, family, etc. These classes are designed to be fun, and for many they may be the only social contact each week. Lip-reading instruction is usually included in rehabilitation programmes and seems to aid confidence to participate in day-to-day life and in developing residual communication skills.

Sign language is the primary mode of communication for many people born deaf. For some others it may be a useful additional aid to communication.

Hearing dogs can offer companionship and become the ears of many deaf people who live alone.

Attendance allowance may be appropriate.

Support agencies   The British Association of the Hard of Hearing (BAHOH) is involved in supporting the Sympathetic Hearing Scheme which aims to make life easier for the thousands of people, both in the UK and elsewhere, who are hearing-impaired. It is a practical scheme providing facilities such as specially adapted telephones to help not only deaf and hard-of-hearing people but also anyone interested enough to support the scheme, such as shops and offices.

BAHOH also has 250 nationwide clubs providing support, advice, and

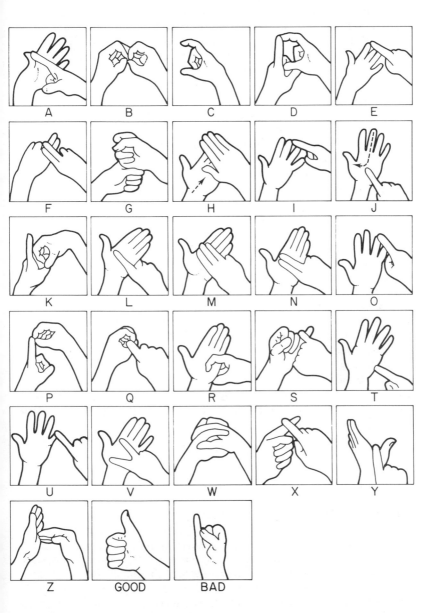

Fig. 7 The standard manual alphabet

friendship. It organises holidays, courses, conferences, etc., and produces a quarterly magazine, *Hark*.

The Royal National Institute for the Deaf (RNID) is concerned with the needs and problems of people of all ages who have varying conditions and degrees of hearing loss. A comprehensive range of personal services is offered, including special residential provision for both rehabilitation and long-term care. The RNID carries out medical, scientific, and technical research into causes, detection, and assessment of hearing disorders. It is also vocal on the formulation of legislation etc. Its information service includes an extensive library with access to the Prestel system, and it also offers advice concerning hearing aids and environmental aids such as those mentioned earlier. The British Tinnitus Association can be contacted through RNID.

The British Deaf Association (BDA) aims to protect and advance the interests of people with severe hearing loss and is specifically concerned with people who are pre-lingually profoundly deaf. Courses are organised for people of all ages. Awards and scholarships for higher education are available, as well as grants to assist those in special need.

The National Deaf Children's Society is the major organisation concerned with hearing-impaired children and their parents. Branches throughout the UK provide guidance on schooling and further education and seek educational and welfare improvements. Its other services and facilities include a home-assistant service for parents, a national holiday scheme, grants to purchase specialised equipment for individuals and schools, bursaries to help train teachers and other professionals concerned with hearing impairment, and a quarterly magazine, *Talk*, along with other literature.

The Royal Association in aid of the Deaf and Dumb (RADD) offers services which include trained staff to act as interpreters, social clubs and recreational facilities, and special social services for those with additional handicaps. These services are available mainly in the south of England.

Other support agencies include the National Council of Social Workers with the Deaf, the Association of Teachers of Lip-reading to Adults, and the British Association of Teachers of the Deaf (BATOD).

Useful literature

● An extensive range of literature is available through the above organisations, some of which is specially designed for students.
● *The right job for you: careers guidance for the hearing impaired*, G. Turner (William Heinemann Medical Books, 1983)
● *I can't hear like you*, Althea (Dinosaur, 1985)
● *Sign language: the study of deaf people and their language*, J.G. Kyle and B. Woll (Cambridge University Press, 1985)
● *The hearing-impaired child in your class* (RNID and BATOD, 1985)

- *Deafness*, J.C. Ballantyne and J.A.M. Martin (Churchill Livingstone, 1984)
- *Hearing impairment: a guide for people with auditory handicaps and those concerned with their care and rehabilitation.* K. Lysons (Woodhead—Faulkner, 1984).
- *Educating hearing-impaired children in ordinary and special schools*, M. Reed (Open University, 1984)
- *Rehabilitation and acquired deafness*, ed. W.J. Watts (Croom Helm, 1983)
- *Louder than words*, J. Hough (Great Ouse Press, 1983)
- *Sign and say books 1 and 2* (RNID, 1981/1984) These booklets contain British, American, and deaf—blind manual alphabets and photographs of about 800 British deaf signs.
- *RNID information directory* (RNID, annual)
- *How to cope with hearing loss*, Kenneth Lysons (Granada, 1980)
- *Can't your child hear?* — *a guide for those who care about deaf children*, Roger D. Freeman, C. Lipteon, F. Carbin, and Robert J. Boese (Croom Helm, 1981)
- *The hearing impaired child and the family*, Michael Nolan and Ivan Tucker (Souvenir Press, 1981)
- *Deaf worlds: a study of integration, segregation and disability*, Sally Sainsbury (Hutchinson Education, 1986)
- *Ways and means vol. 3* — *hearing impairment: a resource book of information, technical aids, teaching materials and methods used in the education of hearing impaired children*, ed. A. Jackson (Macmillan, 1981)

Visual impairment

Introduction   There are about 135 000 people in the UK who are registered blind, but most will have some sight. In addition there are more than 40 000 people who are partially sighted.

People with a visual handicap come from all kinds of background. Some are young; however, most people who are visually handicapped are elderly, having lost their sight as they have grown older. There is a distinction made between severe visual handicap and partial sight.

A person with a visual handicap experiences a great reduction in the ability to gather information about the external environment through the sense of sight. Hearing and touch then play a significant role, as visually handicapped people become more reliant upon these senses.

Main categories   Once a visual disability has been confirmed by a consultant ophthalmologist (and this is usually assessed in co-operation with the family doctor), it is advisable to register with the social services department in order to receive the range of services available both locally and nationally. The Certificate of Registration has to be completed by a consultant ophthalmologist, and there are three main categories of vision: (i) technically blind, (ii) partially sighted, and (iii) partially sighted and entitled to use services appropriate to blind people.

The statutory definition of blindness is 'that a person should be so blind as to be unable to perform any work for which eyesight is essential'. 'Work' in this sense does not only mean paid employment.

There is no statutory definition of partial sight, but, where there is a substantial and permanent handicap by defective vision, then a person can come within the scope of welfare services that local authorities provide for people who are blind. It may be stated on the certificate that the person is likely to become blind soon or that the nature of the visual defect is such that benefit could be gained from training for employment or other services appropriate to a person who is blind. In these circumstances, the person who is partially sighted can be eligible for a greater range of services.

It is important to realise that many people who are registered blind nevertheless have useful amounts of residual vision (that is, some remaining sensitivity to light). On the other hand, many people who have too much sight to be able to register as blind do experience a serious visual handicap. Some of the latter group are categorised as 'partially sighted', but there are probably people with impaired vision who do not appear on any register of visually or other handicapped people.

Causes   The experience of visual loss is very different for those who have become suddenly (adventitiously) blind, who can use their existing knowledge of sight, and for those who are born (congenitally) blind.

Blindness has many causes. Some common causes of visual loss include the following:

● diabetic retinopathy (a general loss of vision, possibly quite sudden, which usually occurs in the 40–60 age group as a result of deterioration of the retina due to long-term diabetes and high blood pressure (hypertension));
● glaucoma (where there is loss of peripheral vision, leaving clear residual central vision until a very late stage);
● cataract (the crystalline lens becomes increasingly opaque and eventually needs to be removed surgically); and

- macular degeneration (where degeneration occurs within the central portion of the retina, resulting in images becoming increasingly ill-defined with a central 'hole' in the vision).

These are the commonest causes of failing vision experienced by people over the age of 60 years. Incidence of short-sightedness and injury are particularly significant in adult working life. Hemianopia involves loss of half of the field of vision, and retinitis pigmentosa is an example of a hereditary condition affecting young adults.

Measles may cause visual impairment, and the virus herpes can dangerously affect eyesight.

Congenital malformations such as result from rubella (German measles) have caused much concern and have increased the emphasis on preventive care in pregnancy. Many congenital conditions are often not amenable to treatment — for example, bilateral optic-nerve atrophy is degenerative and results in cloudy vision.

Diagnosis Every year, some children and adults experience deteriorating sight due to illness, accident, or the progression of a sight defect. The period before and for some time after diagnosis can be a very traumatic time for the whole family.

Families need clarification of the future implications of blindness, practical information, and time to adjust to the ways in which such a handicap may affect their lives. Feelings of guilt, fear, frustration, bereavement, and often very ambivalent emotions will require the support of others in the family together with specialist help.

An individual's personal and emotional resources are a major factor in successful adjustment to a visual handicap. Strong support from family and friends, secure and adequate income, and reasonable prospects of employment are important additional factors.

Treatment Surgery may be possible for a few conditions (cataract, for example). Ophthalmological aids are particularly valuable for those people who are partially sighted, but they are rarely successful without additional support in terms of learning new techniques (for example hand—eye co-ordination), educational and social rehabilitation, and personal adjustment.

Regular assessment is especially important for those people with some visual ability.

Exercise Many people — even those with severe visual impairment — have been able to participate in a whole variety of sports and leisure activities. Skiing, canoeing, and horse-riding are just some examples. Society in general has tended to be unnecessarily protective towards people who are visually handicapped and to assume that they must be dependent on others.

Family living   Parents will need to encourage a visually handicapped baby to move about and to explore the environment. As children get older, parents should encourage independence inside the home and support the child when he or she is exploring a new environment elsewhere. Some parents find it hard to overcome fears for their child's safety, but being overprotective does not help the visually handicapped child to learn and to grow in confidence.

For most people with a visual handicap, mobility, reading, and interpersonal communication provide difficulties. The spoken word is important but, being unable to identify someone by sight, it is not easy to begin a conversation and appear confident. Verbal communication can thus be greatly inhibited unless others in the sighted world help with introductions and give verbal clues to conversation. Many people feel that visual impairment restricts their social opportunities more than the nature of the handicap inevitably requires. Mobility officers employed by the social services department can assist.

The Royal National Institute for the Blind (RNIB) has education advisors who are qualified teachers and can help and support parents with their very young children, particularly during their first two years. Assessment of a child's progress in babyhood through to pre-school age is important and may involve the paediatrician, educational psychologist, and social worker in the child development centre or special medical unit.

The RNIB also runs specialist nursery schools which are particularly helpful to those children who have additional physical and mental handicaps.

The RNIB's 'Talking Book' library of books recorded on tape, and the ever increasing range of literature and magazines available in Braille or Moon (raised characters read by the fingers) in local libraries, greatly helps reduce the isolation of a blind person from the visual world. Assistance with provision of radio and television is also available.

Local authorities have a responsibility to provide residential accommodation for all elderly or handicapped people in need. Demand for more specialised accommodation is in fact increasing, because of the growing number of elderly and infirm people in general, many of whom are visually handicapped. However, integrated care is more widely available and therefore staff and other residents need to be aware of the specific problems of the visually handicapped.

Education   Few children are totally blind. Children with a visual impairment need extra help and support at school, and a growing number attend or continue to attend their local school, with specialist back-up. It is advantageous for the child to live among his or her family and friends.

However, some children who are visually handicapped may be unable to learn through education by ordinary teaching methods. Children who have very little or no sight are taught in a different way from children who are partially sighted and may more beneficially attend schools where access to special teaching programmes can be more effectively provided. Schools for the blind can offer guidance and assessment, and parents may visit a school before making a decision as to which resource would be best for their child. Some children may have additional handicaps or their learning may be affected in other ways — if their visual handicap has been the result of cerebral injury, for example.

The Education Act 1981 requires that a statement of each child's special educational needs be drawn up, with contributions from a range of specialists, so that the most suitable kind of school can be selected for each child. Ultimately any decision needs to be made with the co-operation of the parents, taking into account individual and family needs.

Most schools for children who are blind are residential, and children generally attend as weekly boarders. Some parents prefer to send their child to nursery classes, playgroups, or even local primary school to begin with but may consider specialist schooling later.

There is a range of schools at secondary level catering for visually impaired children of different academic ability. For example, the RNIB grammar schools at Worcester and Chorleywood prepare pupils for general education examinations and university entrance. Two other schools — St Vincent's (Liverpool) and Tapton Mount (Sheffield) — also have links with mainstream schools. The RNIB Rushton Hall (primary) and Conndover Hall (secondary) schools provide places for children who have other physical and mental handicaps in addition to visual impairment. There are other special residential units for those whose overall disabilities give rise to severe learning difficulties.

Communication is a vital element of education if children are to be part of the community and not be isolated. With the technological advances in recent years, the use of tape-recorders, typewriters, closed-circuit television, computers, etc. has greatly assisted children in learning basic skills. Braille — a system in which characters are represented by raised dots — is learned, and all children are usually given the opportunity to acquire keyboard skills.

For children who are partially sighted, developmental progress in terms of perception and spatial-orientation skills can be difficult. Assimilating the variant qualities of objects, light reflection, colour variation, distance, attitude, angle, etc. may be more problematic for those who are born with a visual impairment.

Further education and training   Careers officers, specialist employment officers, and RNIB officers can contact young people in their last years at school, help them look realistically at their abilities to do certain types of work, and advise about training and further education. Many young people who are visually handicapped attend the RNIB Hethersett College (Reigate) or Queen Alexandra College (Birmingham), which are further-education colleges which also provide guidance on suitable training and employment. These centres work closely with local industrial, social, and educational services.

The Royal National College for the Blind at Hereford offers courses in GCSE and A-level study, office skills, and piano tuning. The RNIB Commercial College (London) runs courses in shorthand, audio-typing, telephony, computer programming, and optacon training (learning to use a machine which provides print in a form which can be read by the fingers), etc. Students can take a three-year course to train as chartered physiotherapists at the North London School of Physiotherapy.

A growing number of further-education colleges are catering for school-leavers with a variety of physical and mental handicaps, but this provision may vary from area to area.

The RNIB provides grants to students in colleges and universities (including the Open University) to help with the extra costs incurred due to a student's visual handicap — for example, Braille equipment, tape-recorders, readers, etc. It runs students Braille and tape libraries which transcribe into Braille or record on to tape academic material for individual students. Some students with defective vision who are not registered as blind may make use of some of these services too.

In all training, it is important that there is always some link between the somewhat protected world of the schools for the blind and the daily life of the sighted world, to encourage and allow independence.

Employment   RNIB services include a nationwide service to help people with commercial and professional qualifications find jobs; help in obtaining special aids at work; and assistance for workers based at home.

It is important that people who experience visual loss later in life do not give up work without specialist consultation. People who are visually handicapped establish careers in business, the main professions, and self-employed concerns, etc. A wide range of special equipment is available to assist people in work, and this can be provided by the Employment Services Division of the Manpower Services Commission. A personal-reader service is also available to visually handicapped people in employment.

One difficulty has been that some employers will not agree to offer a job unless the right equipment is already available or only when such equipment has been shown to be satisfactory. However, special equipment may only be made available once the person has been given the job; thus there is a 'vicious circle'. The RNIB can advise employers at interview stage.

Training, and subsequently work, can be offered in one of the sheltered workshops catering specifically for people with visual loss. Many of these workshops no longer offer only traditional crafts such as basket- and brush-making but also have modern light engineering and assembly processes.

The Employment Services Division of the Manpower Services Commission, through its blind persons resettlement officers and training officers, provides a specialist placement service for people looking for work in industry.

Aids and benefits/Rehabilitation Registration with the social services department is voluntary but can be made only on the recommendation of a consultant ophthalmologist. A registered person is entitled to local and national services and financial help such as additional tax relief and supplementary benefits.

Social services departments can arrange for help in mastering new techniques for daily living, such as shaving, washing, eating, and, most importantly, how to get about on one's own. Two common aids to independent mobility are the long cane and guide-dogs. Some local authorities employ mobility officers and technical officers to visit people at home and help them to learn new methods to cope with everyday life, communications, and getting about.

The RNIB's London resource centre has a wide range of aids, including handy kitchen gadgets, magnifying lenses, and expensive electronic reading equipment. These can be inspected by people with a visual handicap, their relatives, and friends.

For some, residential rehabilitation may be more appropriate. The RNIB runs a residential centre in Torquay. Residents learn new techniques for daily living, to touch type, and to read Braille and Moon. Those people who have some residual vision are encouraged to use it.

Equipment designed to help make life easier includes watches, clocks, pens, and aids for cutting bread and for threading needles. Tactile dials can be fitted to cookers and other domestic equipment. The RNIB sells a wide range of aids and games, such as playing cards and chess, at subsidised prices.

Specialised developments have included the electrosonic torch and ultrasonic spectacles which provide a sound 'profile' of the immediate foreground.

Support agencies The Royal National Institute for the Blind, which was founded in 1868, is the largest organisation of its kind in the world. In addition to funds raised itself, it receives some contributions from national and local government towards some of its many services. These services include an education advisory service, schools and colleges for visually handicapped children and young people, a special unit for deaf—blind children, careers advice, grants, student Braille and tape libraries, specially adapted games, and seaside hotels for low-cost holidays. There is a Resources Centre at Great Portland Street in London where a wide range of aids and items of electronic equipment can be inspected and tried out by people with a visual handicap.

Other agencies providing information and guidance include General Welfare of the Blind, National Library for the Blind, the Partially Sighted Society, The Guide Dogs for the Blind Association, and the Iris Fund for Prevention of Blindness.

Useful literature

● The RNIB provides a wide range of leaflets including:

What is it like to be blind?
Guidelines for teachers and parents of visually handicapped children with additional handicaps
Braille and Moon alphabet cards
Blind and partially sighted students in college
Local authority social rehabilitation services to visually handicapped people

● *Blind man's bluff*, H.J. Hinton (Paul Elek, 1974)
● *Blindness: what it is, what it does, and how to live with it*, T.J. Carroll (Little Brown, 1975)
● *Guidelines for nurses working with visual handicap* (Royal College of Nursing, 1984)
● *Good news for the partially sighted*, Gerry Holloway (Partially Sighted Society)
● *All about glaucoma: questions and answers about people with glaucoma*, Wolfgang Leydhecker and Ronald Pitts Crick (Faber & Faber, 1981)

Retinitis pigmentosa

Introduction   Retinitis pigmentosa (RP) is one of a group of hereditary diseases which affect the retina — the light-sensitive tissue inside the eye in which the first stages of seeing by the brain take place. 'Retinitis' implies a disease of the retina, and 'pigmentosa' refers to the characteristic lumps of dark-brown pigment (melanin) which gradually become more widespread as the disease progresses.

Main characteristics/Treatment   In RP, the retina slowly degenerates and loses its ability to transmit pictures to the brain. Often the first symptom is night blindness — loss of vision in poor light — followed by narrowing of side vision leading to what is often called 'tunnel vision'. The symptoms may occur at any age but most commonly become apparent in teenagers and young adults.

In some cases RP may be associated with other medical conditions, for example Usher's syndrome — a hereditary condition in which severe visual loss develops after an initial hearing impairment.

At present there is no treatment which has been shown to arrest the progress of RP or cure it.

Inheritance pattern   All types of RP are inherited and they fall into three main categories, depending on the mode of transmission:

i) The recessive type can strike without warning in a family with no recent previous history of visual handicap and can affect members of either sex. It is estimated that one person in 80 carries the gene for recessive RP, and there is as yet no way to detect these carriers.

ii) The dominant type usually appears in every generation of an affected family. A person with this type has a 1 in 2 chance of having an affected child with each birth.

iii) The sex-linked type affects males only and is transmitted by female carriers to their sons. There is a 1 in 2 chance of having an affected male child. Female carriers of the sex-linked type are detectable. Affected men with sex-linked RP cannot transmit the condition to their sons.

Family living   Perhaps because the condition is relatively uncommon, families are often not given enough information about RP following diagnosis. Opportunities to discuss the implications of the condition and to understand what to expect as it progresses may not be available. Some people may find the progressive nature of the condition particularly frightening and frustrating — each day, a person may see less and less of his or her family and environment.

Families need more support and help from the services in the hospital and community. Contact with other families is an important source of information and support and can be vital to adjustment.

People with RP find that public ignorance concerning the physical and emotional problems which they face is an additional handicap.

Support agencies   The British Retinitis Pigmentosa Society, formed in 1975, provides literature concerning RP and guidance and support to individuals and their families. It has a number of local groups in Britain.

Hearing and visual impairment

Introduction   It is not known how many people in the UK have the dual handicap of visual and hearing impairments, but the number is estimated to be in the region of 6000 or more.

A person who has both a visual and a hearing handicap is very isolated and lonely. The finger-spelling or manual-alphabet system is often the only way in which any communication can be achieved with other people. This is where the 'speaker's' fingers are placed at different points on the hand of the 'listener' to indicate different letters of the alphabet.

Causes   Most people who are deaf—blind are elderly, initially acquiring one handicap and then developing the other through age. A few may acquire the double handicap as a result of injury or illness.

Children may be born with deaf—blindness due to various causes:

● Maternal rubella (German measles) may result in a child having a hearing and visual impairment with other disabilities such as heart defects and mental handicap.
● Usher's syndrome (retinitis pigmentosa plus deafness) and Norrey's syndrome are hereditary conditions where there is an initial hearing impairment and a severe visual loss develops.
● Meningitis can cause impairment to the hearing and visual senses together with possible brain damage.

Diagnosis/Treatment   The ease of adjustment to the disability depends to some extent on the severity of the handicap, the age of onset, and the communication skills developed before the dual handicap became apparent.

A person who is potentially likely to lose a second sense needs to become familiar with the manual-alphabet system, but in some situations a person may be reluctant to admit that the additional disability is occurring and may need help with emotional and psychological barriers already being experienced.

At whatever age a person becomes both deaf and blind, it is clearly a devastating experience. Skilled guidance is needed in aiding mobility and communication.

Preservation of speech, where it already exists, is of vital importance, but speech therapy is frequently not available to meet the needs of people with this kind of disability.

Education   For a child with early hearing and visual impairment there

Fig. 8 The deaf—blind manual alphabet, designed for use with those whose understanding can be reached only through the sense of touch. The left hand is that of the deaf—blind person; the right that of the 'speaker', pressed firmly against it.

may be extremely slow progress in learning. Concept realisation may be particularly difficult. Most children attend schools for children with severe or moderate learning difficulties.

As there is no form of training on deaf — blindness available in the UK, there are very few teachers qualified to teach children who have both visual and hearing impairment. The irony is that if a child has only a hearing impairment or only a visual impairment, the education authorities can provide qualified advisors and specialist school provision. However, the RNIB and SENSE provide advisory teachers and a few places are available in specialist schools.

Family living Many deaf — blind people feel too disheartened to persevere with communication except on a very simple level. However, the manual-alphabet system is in fact easy to learn and could thus be used by professionals, carers, family, and friends.

A person with this dual handicap requires a great deal of encouragement in order to participate in everyday life. Some feel that they are or have become misfits in society. It is thus important that the person is encouraged to seek new experiences, and to use initiative where possible. A good working relationship with one person in particular is valuable.

In most large cities, voluntary organisations will run a club specifically for people with deaf — blindness. In addition, the RNIB, the National Deaf — Blind Helpers' League, and SENSE offer specialised holidays.

Employment/Rehabilitation There are a few rehabilitation centres which may accept people who are deaf — blind but there are five units (in Harrogate, Bath, Market Deeping, Glasgow, and Birmingham) which cater specifically for this dual handicap. The National Deaf — Blind Helpers' League also runs flats to aid rehabilitation of people with dual handicap.

Employment opportunities may be appropriate within open or sheltered employment. Many people have additional handicaps which mean that they may have to consider a day centre or a home-worker scheme.

Mobility This is a major problem, providing many restrictions. It is very difficult for people with a visual/hearing handicap to consider going out alone and they will almost always need a guide or helper to accompany them. This has obvious limitations in terms of independence.

Aids and benefits Because of the relatively small number of deaf — blind people registered as disabled (in the region of 1000 in the UK), services available tend to be restricted. Registration is made under the heading of 'visually handicapped' and the same categories apply.

The range of aids is similar to that available for people with a visual or hearing loss, but there is a special telephone developed for people with the dual handicap. The Hasicom Council telephone provides communication for those with hearing and sight impairment using a network of Braille terminals via an ordinary telephone connection.

Further information on relevant aids and benefits is given in the sections for hearing impairment and visual impairment.

Support agencies   The Royal National Institute for the Blind has an advisor for the deaf – blind. It also publishes a booklet, *Will you help the deaf-blind?*

The National Deaf – Blind Helpers' League has a leaflet called *How to talk to a deaf – blind person* which shows how to learn the manual alphabet.

The Royal Association in aid of the Deaf and Dumb has specialists to work with people with this dual handicap in their homes, hospitals, or residential homes.

SENSE – The National Deaf – Blind and Rubella Association – also offers useful information, has specialist advisors, and provides a wide variety of services for deaf – blind people.

The Royal National Institute for the Deaf publishes a leaflet on *The deaf – blind manual alphabet*.

Useful literature

- *Christopher: a silent life*, Margaret Brook (Bedford Square Press, 1984)
- *The deaf – blind baby: a programme of care*, Peggy Freeman, (William Heinemann Medical Books, 1985)
- *Understanding the deaf – blind child*, Peggy Freeman (William Heinemann Medical Books, 1975)

Kinetic impairment

The kinetic sense, which deals with balance, is located in the cerebellum (the part of the brain lying below the cerebral hemisphere). Disability can be caused by damage of the cerebellum due to trauma, tumours, or degeneration, etc. Usually the activities of the cerebellum are carried out without intruding on consciousness, but, if the cerebellum is damaged, there may be symptoms of vertigo, staggering gait, tremors, and an inability to assess the weight of an object when handling it.

Muscular movements — especially those requiring fine co-ordination — can also be affected, as nerves from joints and muscles lead to the cerebellum.

Tactile impairment

The skin has millions of cutaneous nerves that convey to the cerebral part of the brain the sense of touch, pain, and temperature (heat and cold). Tactile sensation is most marked in the palm and fingertips, and less so on certain areas such as the back.

Localised skin damage, such as a severe burn, may be viewed as a major disability in, for example, a professional such as a musician. There are also certain diseases or disorders of the brain and spinal cord that cause loss of sensation of touch, pain, and temperature.

Olfactory and gustatory impairment

The sense of smell is known as the olfactory sense and the sense of taste as the gustatory sense. These senses are, for practical purposes, inter-related. The host of innumerable tastes is lost if the sense of smell is blocked.

The sense of taste is rarely affected on its own, although this can happen after a head injury. The back third of the tongue (served by the ninth cranial nerve) detects bitterness, and the front two-thirds of the tongue (served by the fifth cranial nerve) detects sweetness and sourness.

The sense of smell can likewise be affected after a head injury. A severe cold will also cause a temporary loss of smell, although this cannot be classed as a disability.

Addresses of support agencies

- **Action for Research into Multiple Sclerosis (ARMS)**
  4A Chapel Hill, Stanstead, Essex CM24 8AG (0279 815553)

- **Age Concern**
  Bernard Sunley House, Pitcairn Road, Mitcham, Surrey CR4 3LL
  (01−640 5431)

- **AID**
  See Assistance and Independence for Disabled People

- **Alzheimer's Disease Society**
  3rd Floor, Bank Buildings, Fulham Broadway, London SW6 1EP
  (01−381 3177)

- **ARMS**
  See Action for Research into Multiple Sclerosis

- **The Arthritis and Rheumatism Council**
  41 Eagle Street, London WC1R 4AR (01−405 8572)

- **Arthritis Care**
  6 Grosvenor Crescent, London SW1X 7ER (01−235 0902)

- **ASBAH**
  See Association for Spina Bifida and Hydrocephalus

- **Assistance and Independence for Disabled People (AID)**
  182 Brighton Road, Coulsdon, Surrey CR3 2NF (01−645 9014)

- **Association to Aid the Sexual and Personal Relationships of the
  Disabled (SPOD)**
  286 Camden Road, London N7 OBJ (01−607 8851)

- **Association of Carers**
  Medway Homes, Balfour Road, Rochester, Kent ME4 6QU
  (0634 813981)

- **Association to Combat Huntington's Chorea (COMBAT)**
  Borough House, 34a Station Road, Hinckley, Leics LE10 1AP
  (0455 615558)

  and Patient Welfare at

  108 Battersea High Street, London SW11 3HP (01 – 223 7000)

- **Association of Crossroads Care Attendent Schemes Ltd**
  94 Coton Road, Rugby CV21 4LN (0788 73653)

- **Association of Disabled Professionals**
  The Stables, 73 Pound Road, Banstead, Surrey SM7 2HU
  (07373 52366)

- **Association for Spina Bifida and Hydrocephalus**
  22 Upper Woburn Place, London WC1H 0EP (01 – 388 1382)

- **Association of Teachers of Lip-reading to Adults**
  (Mrs M. Williams) The Police Cottage, Green Rd, Wivelsfield
  Green, Sussex RH17 7QD (0444 84257)

- **Asthma Society and Friends of the Asthma Research Council**
  300 Upper Street, London N1 2XX (01 – 226 2260)

- **British Association of the Hard of Hearing (BAHOH)**
  7 – 11 Armstrong Road, London W3 7JL (01 – 743 1110)

- **British Association of Myasthenics**
  (Mrs M.E. Rivett) 9 Potters Drive, Mariners Park, Hopton, Norfolk
  NR31 9RW (0502 731904)

- **British Association of Teachers of the Deaf**
  The Rycroft Centre, Royal Schools for the Deaf, Stanley Road,
  Cheadle Hulme, Cheadle, Cheshire SK8 6RF (061 – 437 5951)

- **British Computer Society's Specialist Group for the Disabled**
  13 Mansfield Street, London W1M 0BP (01 – 637 0471)

- **British Deaf Association (BDA)**
  38 Victoria Place, Carlisle, Cumbria CA1 1HU (0228 48844)

- **British Diabetic Association**
  10 Queen Anne Street, London W1M 0BD (01 – 323 1531)

- **British Dyslexia Association**
  Church Lane, Peppard, Oxon RG9 5JN (049 17 699)

- **British Epilepsy Association**
  Crowthorne House, New Wokingham Road, Wokingham, Berks
  RG11 3AY (0344 773122)

● **British Heart Foundation**
102 Gloucester Place, London W1H 4DH (01 – 935 0185)

● **British Paraplegic Sports Society**
Harvey Road, Aylesbury, Bucks HP21 8PP (0296 84848)

● **The British Polio Fellowship**
Bell Close, West End Road, Ruislip, Middx HA4 6LP (0895 675515)

● **The British Red Cross Society**
9 Grosvenor Crescent, London SW1X 7EJ (01 – 235 5454)

● **British Retinitis Pigmentosa Society**
Greens Norton Court, Greens Norton, Towcester, Northants
NN12 8BS (0327 53276)

● **British Sports Association for the Disabled**
Hayward House, Barnard Crescent, Aylesbury, Bucks HP21 8PP
(0296 27889)

● **British Tinnitus Association**
c/o Royal National Institute for the Deaf (*see below*)

● **Brittle Bone Society**
112 City Road, Dundee DD2 2PW (0382 67603)

● **The Chest, Heart and Stroke Association**
Tavistock House North, Tavistock Square, London WC1H 9JE
(01 – 387 3012)

● **The Coeliac Society of the United Kingdom**
PO Box 220, High Wycombe, Bucks HP11 2HY (0494 37278)

● **COMBAT**
See Association to Combat Huntington's Chorea

● **Compassionate Friends**
6 Denmark Street, Bristol BS1 5DQ (0272 292778)

● **Contact a Family**
16 Strutton Ground, London SW1P 2HP (01 – 222 2695)

● **Counsel and Care for the Elderly**
131 Middlesex Street, London E1 7JF (01 – 621 1624)

● **The Cystic Fibrosis Research Trust**
Alexandra House, 5 Blyth Road, Bromley, Kent BR1 3RS
(01 – 464 7211)

● **Dial UK Limited**
Dial House, 117 High Street, Claycross, Chesterfield, Derbyshire
S45 9DZ (0246 864498)

- **DIG**
  See Disablement Income Group Charitable Trust

- **Disability Alliance**
  25 Denmark Street, London WC2 8NJ (01 — 240 0806)

- **Disabled Drivers Association**
  Ashwellthorpe, Norwich NR16 1EX (050841 449)

- **Disabled Living Foundation**
  380 — 384 Harrow Road, London W9 2HU (01 — 289 6111)

- **Disablement Income Group Charitable Trust (DIG)**
  Attlee House, 28 Commercial Street, London E1 6LR
  (01 — 247 2138)

- **Down's Syndrome Association**
  1st Floor, 12 — 13 Clapham Common Southside, London SW4 7AA
  (01 — 720 0008)

- **Dyslexia Institute**
  133 Gresham Road, Staines TW18 2AJ (0784 59498)

- **Family Fund**
  PO Box 50, York YO1 1UY (0904 21115)

- **Friedreich's Ataxia Group**
  Burleigh Lodge, Knowle Lane Cranleigh, Surrey GU6 8RD
  (0483 272741)

- **General Welfare of the Blind**
  37 — 55 Ashburton Grove, London N7 7DW (01 — 609 0206)

- **Greater London Association for Disabled People (GLAD)**
  336 Brixton Road, London SW9 7AA (01 — 274 0107)

- **The Guide Dogs for the Blind Association**
  9 — 11 Park Street, Windsor, Berks SL4 1JR (0753 855711)

- **The Haemophilia Society**
  123 Westminster Bridge Road, London SE1 7HR (01 — 928 2020)

- **Helen Arkell Dyslexia Centre**
  14 Crondace Road, London SW6 4BB (01 — 736 0748)

- **Help the Aged**
  St James's Walk, London EC1R 0BE (01 — 253 0253)

- **Holiday Care Service**
  2 Old Bank Chambers, Station Road, Horley, Surrey RH6 9HW
  (029 34 74535)

- **The Hornsby Centre**
  71 Wandsworth Common Westside, London SW18 2ED
  (01—871 2691)

- **Hyperactive Children's Support Group**
  59 Meadowside, Angmering, Littlehampton, West Sussex
  BN16 4BW (0903 725182)

- **Invalid Children's Aid Association (ICAA)**
  126 Buckingham Palace Road, London SW1W 9SB (01—730 9891)

- **Iris Fund for Prevention of Blindness**
  York House, 199 Westminster Bridge Road, London SE1 7UT
  (01—928 7743)

- **Kith & Kids**
  Chestnut Cottage, Stanstead Road, Hunsdon, Herts SG12 8PZ
  (0920 870741)

- **Lady Hoare Trust**
  c/o Arthritis Care (*see above*)

- **Leukaemia Research Fund**
  43 Great Ormond Street, London WC1N 3JJ (01—405 0101)

- **The Leukaemia Care Society**
  PO Box 82, Exeter, Devon EX2 5DP (0392 218514)

- **Lupus Group**
  c/o Arthritis Care (*see above*)

- **Mencap**
  See Royal Society for Mentally Handicapped Children and Adults

- **Mobility Information Service**
  National Mobility Centre, MOTEC, High Ercall, Telford, Shropshire TF6 6RB (0952 770881)

- **Motability**
  Boundary House, 91—93 Charterhouse Street, London EC1M 6BT
  (01—253 1211)

- **Motor Neurone Disease Association**
  61 Derngate, Northampton NN1 1UE (0604 250505)

- **The Multiple Sclerosis Society**
  25 Effie Road, London SW6 1EE (01—736 6267)

- **Muscular Dystrophy Group of Great Britain and Northern Ireland**
  Nattrass House, 35 Macaulay Road, London SW4 0QP
  (01—720 8055)

- **The National Ankylosing Spondylitis Society**
  6 Grosvenor Crescent, London SW1X 7ER (01—235 9585)

- **National Association for the Relief of Paget's Disease**
  (Mrs A. Stanfield) 413 Middleton Road, Middleton, Manchester
  M24 4QZ (061—643 1998)

- **National Association for Remedial Education**
  2 Lichfield Road, Stafford ST17 4JX (0785 46872)

- **The National Autistic Society**
  276 Willesden Lane, London NW2 5RB (01—451 3844)

- **National Bureau for Handicapped Students**
  336 Brixton Road, London SW9 7AA (01—274 0565)

- **National Research Centre for Down's Syndrome**
  9 Westbourne Road, Birmingham B15 5TN (021—454 3126)

- **National Children's Bureau**
  8 Wakley Street, London EC1V 7QE (01—278 9441)

- **National Council for Carers and their Elderly Dependants**
  29 Chilworth Mews, London W2 3RG (01—262 1451)

- **National Council of Social Workers with the Deaf**
  c/o St Vincent Centre for the Deaf, Tobago Street, Glasgow,
  G40 2RH (041—554 8897)

- **National Council for Voluntary Organisations (NCVO)**
  26 Bedford Square, London WC1B 3HU (01—636 4066)

- **The National Deaf—Blind Helpers' League**
  18 Rainbow Court, Paston Ridings, Peterborough PE4 6UP
  (0733 73511)

- **The National Deaf—Blind and Rubella Association (SENSE)**
  311 Gray's Inn Road, London WC1X 8PT (01—278 1005)

- **National Deaf Children's Society**
  45 Hereford Road, London W2 5AH (01—229 9272)

- **National Eczema Society**
  Tavistock House North, Tavistock Square, London WC1H 9SR
  (01—388 4097)

- **National Library for the Blind**
  Cromwell Road, Bredbury, Stockport SK6 2SG (061—494 0217)

- **National Society for Epilepsy**
  Chalfont Centre, Chalfont St Peter, Gerrards Cross, Bucks SL9 0RJ
  (024 07 3991)

- **The National Society for Phenylketonuria and Allied Disorders Limited (NSPKU)**
  26 Towngate Grove, Mirfield, West Yorkshire WF14 9JF
  (0924 492873)

- **Opportunities for the Disabled**
  1 Bank Building, Princes Street, London EC2R 8EU (01 — 726 4963)

- **Organisation for Sickle Cell Anaemia Research (OSCAR)**
  22 Pellatt Grove, London N22 5PL (01 — 889 3300)

- **Parkinson's Disease Society**
  36 Portland Place, London W1N 3DG (01 — 323 1174)

- **Partially Sighted Society**
  c/o Royal National Institute for the Blind (*see below*)

- **People First of London and Thames**
  c/o Kings Fund Centre, 126 Albert Street, London NW1 7NF
  (01 — 267 6111)

- **Physically Handicapped and Able Bodied (PHAB)**
  Tavistock House North, Tavistock Square, London WC1H 9HX
  (01 — 388 1963)

- **Psoriasis Association**
  7 Milton Street, Northampton NN2 7JG (0604 711129)

- **RADAR**
  See Royal Association for Disability and Rehabilitation

- **Rehabilitation Engineering Movement Advisory Group (REMAP)**
  c/o Royal Association for Disability and Rehabilitation (*see below*)

- **Royal Association in aid of the Deaf and Dumb (RADD)**
  27 Old Oak Road, London W3 7HN (01 — 743 6187)

- **Royal Association for Disability and Rehabilitation (RADAR)**
  25 Mortimer Street, London W1N 8AB (01 — 637 5400)

- **Royal National Institute for the Blind (RNIB)**
  224 Great Portland Street, London W1N 6AA (01 — 388 1266)

- **The Royal National Institute for the Deaf (RNID)**
  105 Gower Street, London WC1E 6AH (01 — 387 8033)

- **Royal Society for Mentally Handicapped Children and Adults (Mencap)**
  123 Golden Lane, London EC1Y 0RT (01 — 253 9433)

- **SENSE**
  See The National Deaf — Blind and Rubella Association

- **SEQUAL**
  See Special Equipment and Aids for Living

- **Sickle Cell Society**
  Green Lodge, Barretts Green Road, London NW10 7AP
  (01−961 7795)

- **The Spastics Society**
  12 Park Crescent, London W1N 4EQ (01−636 5020)

  and Family Services and Assessment Centre at

  16 Fitzroy Square, London W1P 5HQ (01−387 9571)

- **Special Equipment and Aids for Living (SEQUAL)**
  Block 178, Milton Trading Estate, Abingdon, Oxon OX14 4ES
  (0235 833193)

- **Spinal Injuries Association**
  Yeoman House, 76 St James's Lane, London N10 3DF
  (01−444 2121)

- **SPOD**
  See Association to Aid the Sexual and Personal Relationships of the
  Disabled

- **Toy Aids**
  Lodbourne Farmhouse, Lodbourne, Gillingham, Dorset SP8 4EH
  (074 76 2256)

- **Tuberous Sclerosis Association of Great Britain**
  (Mrs A. Underhill) Martell Mount, Holywell Road, Malvern Wells,
  Worcs WR14 4LF (06845 63150)

- **VOCAL**
  See Voluntary Organisations Communication and Language

- **Voluntary Council for Handicapped Children**
  c/o National Children's Bureau (*see above*)

- **Voluntary Organisations Communication and Language (VOCAL)**
  336 Brixton Road, London SW9 7AA (01−274 4029)

Index